THE SUPERNATURAL POWER OF HONOR

Discover Breakthrough, Fulfillment, Restoration, and Favor

BEN LIM

BroadStreet
PUBLISHING

BroadStreet Publishing® Group, LLC
Savage, Minnesota, USA
BroadStreetPublishing.com

The Supernatural Power of Honor: Discover Breakthrough, Fulfillment, Restoration, and Favor

9781424570621 (softcover)
9781424570638 (ebook)

Literary agent, Cheryl Ricker of Dunamis Words: Light Your World, www.CherylRicker.com

Cover and interior by Garborg Design Works | garborgdesign.com

Printed in China

26 27 28 29 30 5 4 3 2 1

For Danny Silk, who set the standard for modeling a culture of honor in his generation and still does.

For my father, who taught me the lost art of honor by walking it out in humility.

For Cheryl Ricker, who consistently believed in me and walked with me.

Dr. Ben Lim does it again! An anointed, trusted voice to the nations, God has used Dr. Lim to bring a crucial message to this generation on the way forward via the lost art of honor. Page after page of timeless inspiration and sound doctrine pour out of his book *The Supernatural Power of Honor*! In a darkened world, the message of Jesus speaks a better word, and the message of honor speaks a better way! This book is a must-read for every Christian. A valuable, anointed book to be treasured and read, again and again!

—**Dr. JoLynne Whittaker,** JoLynne Whittaker Ministries,
author of *Date with Destiny*, www.jolynnewhittaker.org

Ben Lim gets it! Honor isn't just something we strive for; it's part of our spiritual DNA as born-again believers. When we were made new in Christ, honor was woven into our identity, not as something to be earned but as something to live out and develop through him. In Ben's *The Supernatural Power of Honor*, he unpacks the biblical foundation of honor—not as the world defines it but as heaven sees it. True honor isn't about self-promotion; it's about self-sacrifice, humility, and serving others. It's about stepping into the finished work of Christ, fully embracing what he has already accomplished and walking in the authority that comes from surrendering to him. This isn't just another book—it's a prophetic wake-up call for this generation.

—**Georgian Banov,** president and cofounder of Global Celebration and
GCSSM Online Ministry and Leadership School,
author of *Joy! God's Secret Weapon for Every Believer*

Ben Lim's *The Supernatural Power of Honor* is a practical, heartfelt journey through the multifacets of honor. Ben's in-depth approach teaches us what honor is, what honor does, and how we can apply it in our lives. He lays out seven core values of honor, a framework we all can benefit from. Honor is not lost, and this book will give you all the tools you need to restore honor in your life. I highly recommend this book!

—**Steve Swanson,** Friends of the Bridegroom Worship Ministries

My good friend, Dr. Ben Lim, is a man of tremendous honor. He takes honor seriously, and it shows in just about everything he endeavors to do. In his new book *The Supernatural Power of Honor*, Dr. Lim expounds on the various facets of honor as they relate to the kingdom of God and the world at large. He is very transparent in regard to showing his wounds, thereby helping his readers see how dishonor can negatively affect the lives of believers and how honor can do so positively. He also provides multiple strategies you can use to become a man or woman of honor. I highly recommend this book!

—**Dr. John Veal,** CEO of John Veal Ministries, author of *Supernaturally Prophetic* and *Supernaturally Delivered*, www.Johnveal.org

Honor is an essential key for this generation to properly step into their destiny. It is more than just high esteem. It is chivalry, honesty, compassion, admiration, and respect for one another and the Lord. Honor is about relationship. It builds a bridge that connects you to what the other person has access to. So when you learn to honor well, the doors of opportunity will open up wide to you. When we understand how to honor each other, we also learn how to love each other well. Ben Lim's *The Supernatural Power of Honor* will teach you how to walk in a place of humility that will make room for your destiny. Let this book take you on a beautiful journey discovering who the Lord is in you and how honor will set you up for your divine purpose.

—**Natasha Hinn,** minister and worship artist,
cofounder of Jesus Army Bootcamp, jesusarmybootcamp.com

The Supernatural Power of Honor, written by my dear friend Ben Lim, will unlock and unleash revelation in how to establish a culture of honor in your Jesus community. Your church, business, ministry, home, and heart will experience moves of the Holy Ghost that can only be demonstrated in an environment that honors him and the prophets or vessels he is using. This book is a word from God from a man of God. Ben Lim walks in the power of God and is one of the greatest examples of honor! When you honor someone, you unlock the grace and power they carry.

If you want to see the potential of those around you maximized, make this book—*The Supernatural Power of Honor*—a must-read!

—**Eddie James,** worship artist; founder of Eddie James Ministries, Eddie James Productions, DreamLife, Fresh Wine Records, and Fresh Wine Publishing; eddiejames.com

Culture is in a famine of character, and one of the central ways we can overcome this famine is by reinstilling honor in ourselves and others. Ben Lim has a unique story and ministry which has created a framework to teach and impart a new understanding of honor that will become part of your operating system when you read it. Through a very personal telling of his journey as well as a fresh look at Scripture, *The Supernatural Power of Honor* will bring much healing and help instill a real sense of God's honor to your life.

—**Shawn Bolz,** minister, author, speaker, TV host, www.bolzministries.com

Ben Lim, a distinguished servant of God, is a prophetic and apostolic voice in our generation. His commitment to the gospel and profound insights into spiritual matters have left an indelible mark on the lives of many. His latest book, *The Supernatural Power of Honor*, is a transformative guide that beautifully articulates the biblical principles of honor, shedding light on its supernatural power to usher believers into a realm of divine blessings and spiritual growth. Lim's teachings encourage readers to appreciate the spiritual inheritance that flows through honoring those who have paved the way for the move of God. His teachings go beyond theoretical concepts, offering practical insights that can be applied in our daily walk with Christ. I wholeheartedly recommend *The Supernatural Power of Honor* to individuals and congregations seeking to deepen their understanding of honor and its transformative impact on spiritual impartation.

—**Apostle Tracy Allen Cooke,** Cooke Revivals Ministries, Inc., Cookerevivals.org

As I read Dr. Lim's *The Supernatural Power of Honor*, I thought of something I heard a wise old speaker once say: "The new broom sweeps clean, but the old broom knows where to sweep!" This book sweeps the corners that others miss. Dr. Lim covers every aspect of the intriguing subject of honor. Lim teaches us how to increase and prosper by utilizing honor as a form of spiritual currency in the unseen world.

—**Dr. Lance Wallnau,** host of the *Lance Wallnau Show*; shared platforms with Ben Carson, Mike Pompeo, Ken Blanchard, and John Maxwell; spoken at the United Nations, Harvard, and London School of Theology; author of *God's Chaos Code*; lancewallnau.com

Too often, we overcomplicate things like hearing God's voice and being led by him, leaving us confused and doubting instead of moving forward into all that he has for us. In this practical new book, Ben Lim gives us the tools we need to discern the voice of God and discover honor on a different level so we can walk in even deeper relationship with him.

—**Kimberly Jones,** Real Talk Kim, senior pastor of Limitless Church, author of *Unsuck,* appeared on *Preachers of Atlanta, Dr. Oz, Chatter Talk Show, BET,* and *Nightline News,* realtalkkim.com

Ben Lim is radically in love with the presence of God. Over all the years I have known him and the events we have done together, he has been one of the kindest and most generous people I have had the pleasure of meeting. He is all in for helping people encounter the glory and majesty of Jesus Christ through the indwelling of the Holy Spirit. I hope his book, *The Supernatural Power of Honor*, will, like Ben's life, encourage you to go deeper into the knowledge of God.

—**Jake Hamilton,** founder of The Fight, www.thisisthefight.com

In a world often devoid of honor, my dear friend's new book *The Supernatural Power of Honor* offers a powerful and timely remedy. This book dismantles misconceptions surrounding honor, illuminating its intrinsic connection to spiritual revival and restoration desperately needed within the body of Christ. Through meticulous exploration of Scripture and passionate storytelling, Dr. Ben not only highlights the significance of honor in the Christian life but also offers a tangible roadmap for experiencing it personally. I believe this book holds the potential to transform individuals, families, and communities, and I wholeheartedly encourage everyone to read it.

—**Leon DuPreez,** senior pastor and founder of Encounter Church, South Africa, author of *The Mystery of the Addereth*, leondupreez.com

Dr. Ben Lim has given us a roadmap for wielding honor in his book *The Supernatural Power of Honor*. Honor opens doors to favor and the miraculous—both blessings which Ben walks in. I am excited to see how the revelations in this book will open doors for you, his readers, to also experience breakthrough as you walk in higher levels of honor.

—**Dawna De Silva,** founder and coleader of Bethel Sozo, author of several books including *Sozo: Saved, Healed and Delivered* and *Overcoming Fear*

The Supernatural Power of Honor by Ben Lim is an incredible and timely message from the Holy Spirit to touch the church and bring it back to the biblical values and principles of the kingdom. This book will touch you, transform you, and put you back in God's perfect will for your life.

—**Evangelist John Ramirez,** ex-Satanist turned evangelist, author of the bestselling book *Fire Prayers*, featured on *Fox News Channel*, *700 Club*, and *Daystar*, johnramirez.org

The Bible constantly links honoring to miracle power. As you read *The Supernatural Power of Honor*, Ben Lim will take you on a journey of discovering how honor releases the power of God and brings blessing!

—**Evangelist Matt Cruz,** author of *Stormproof*, mattcruzministries.com

Contents

Honor: A Lost Art? 13

1 What Is Honor? 23

2 Where'd the Honor Go? 45

3 A Culture of Honor 63

4 Honor: Heaven's Currency 81

5 A Spirit of Honor 95

6 Vessels of Honor 113

7 Honoring the Anointing 126

8 Double Honor 145

9 Dispelling Dishonor 163

10 Honor: A Prophet's Reward 183

Afterword: Honor Activations and Declarations 207

Acknowledgments 232

About the Author 233

Endnotes 235

Honor: A Lost Art?

Honor all people. Love the brotherhood. Fear God.
Honor the king.

1 PETER 2:17 NKJV

Lift your eyes—here comes the overlooked and underestimated, the scarred and steadfast. Crowned by fire, steady through grace, marked with purpose. They don't demand honor—they embody it. Heaven sees them, calls them, and celebrates them.

CHERYL A. RICKER

This book is my life's message.

Who am I to write a book on honor? You might be asking that about me. Haven't Danny Silk, John Bevere, and Kenneth Copeland already done a bang-up job of it? Of course they have. And yet, there's always more when it comes to the kingdom of God; there's always a new facet of his character to be revealed, generation after generation. So who am I? I'm just someone who has paid a high price to walk the narrow road of honor—and I've found honor to be essential for thriving in this kingdom life.

As Dr. Ben Lim, called to be a prophet to the nations, honor has become a key principle in my life and my ministry. Honor is a godly core value, and God has placed a deep desire in me to see people realize it and emulate it. But when you walk in honor as a way of life, as I do, you might be shocked to learn just how few people do the same. I'm not just talking about the whole of the world. I'm referring to a distinct lack of honor in Christian circles that I believe is keeping us from achieving our fullest kingdom potential on the earth.

Honor is all but absent in the modern-day church. Some say it's "lost" on the up-and-coming generations of our day—in particular the millennials (which is my generation) and the Gen Zers. Others wonder if we ever really had it in the first place. Wherever it went, honor is something I believe the church desperately needs. And it's up to these younger generations to reclaim it. Because:

- Where there is honor, there is healing.
- Where there is honor, there is restoration.
- Where there is honor, there is revival.

I've seen honor at work. And friend, I want you to see it too.

You see, when we walk in honor, we walk in the fullness of Christ, emulating his life to the best of our human ability. True Christlikeness is contagious—as is honor when rightly shown among believers.

- Honor is *dignifying*. It values the divine DNA in all people, and it values calling forth the anointings and giftings of the called.
- Honor is *electrifying*. It revives dry bones and makes our hearts leap in our chests by the power of the Spirit.
- Honor is *life-giving*. Because honor originates from the Life-Giver himself, our Creator God.

Before we dive in to rediscover this lost art, allow me to provide you with a bit of context for this message about honor. First and foremost, I need you to know that I believe the Holy Bible is God's complete, inerrant Word and our foundational basis for Christian doctrine. Without this truth, we simply cannot make a case for honor as a biblical imperative.

Second, I believe in the voice of the prophets, the fivefold ministry, and the spiritual gifts of the Holy Spirit. Bring on the signs, wonders, and miracles! I believe these gifts manifest in a wide variety of Spirit-fueled anointings and mantles we are meant to carry and pass on through the generations.

And third and finally, I believe we are saved by grace alone through faith in Jesus Christ—and that this grace-laced reality equips and empowers us to do good kingdom works in response. A works-based theology hinders a spirit of honor because it places value on what you do instead of who you are in Christ.

As you thumb your way through the pages of this humble offering, my prayer is that you would be able to see yourself walking as Jesus did when he was on the earth—as a servant-hearted, swift-footed, everything-laid-down lover of God who accepts responsibility for and takes authority over bridging generational, societal, and cultural gaps in the church and in the world. To help you gain that perspective, you will find some "Honorable Reflections" questions I have included at the end of each chapter for you to think about. In the afterword, I have also included "Honor Activations and Declarations" that will help you apply what you're learning about honor to whatever circumstances you're walking through. As a fellow sojourner, I can testify to the very real, highly practical benefits of walking in honor—benefits that manifest both in the natural and in the supernatural world.

Blessing. Favor. Open doors. And so much more. Not to mention a level of intimacy with God that gives you access to his kingdom secrets here on the earth.

> ***As a fellow sojourner, I can testify to the very real, highly practical benefits of walking in honor—benefits that manifest both in the natural and in the supernatural world.***

Walking in honor has allowed me to embrace my true identity as an image-bearer of the Most High God, made one with him in Christ by the power of the Holy Spirit. This revelation has opened my mind to receive and bestow honor freely, knowing full well that it is an abundant and renewable kingdom resource. Equipped with this powerful tool, I have been uniquely positioned as an instrument of healing, restoration, and reconciliation in this earthly realm.

This story is for the underdogs like me. The ones looking for healing, restoration, and vision. It comes to you through the lens of a fellow emerging leader who is desperately holding onto faith and vigorously fighting for what he believes in—God's Word, God's promises, and God's recompense.

What Honor Is About

Walking in honor isn't about spewing pleasantries, or (God forbid) flatteries. It's about having the mind of Christ and walking in his way. Honor is about doing the difficult thing—the righteous thing—even when nobody is looking. Honor is about going deeper to discover the hidden treasure that will enrich your life and all the lives you touch. Honor is about building—and reinforcing—strong spiritual foundations that will last throughout the generations.

In today's divisive, black-hat-white-hat cancel culture, emerging leaders fight an uphill battle in a war they simply cannot win in their own strength. With fathers and sons, mothers and daughters, elders and emerging leaders turning against one another in competitiveness, fear, and an undeniable orphan spirit, I believe the Millennial Generation will be the one to reclaim honor for its own and give it all back to God in faith. In fact, anyone of any generation can do this, but it takes a recognition of what has been lost and a determination to reclaim and rebuild it.

You may be wondering, *If honor is a lost art, where did it go?* How can we reclaim it—and bridge the gap between the generations?

Embracing honor as a kingdom virtue—and as a spiritual imperative for the kingdom of God—means embracing an upside-down life in the natural world…one where the last is first, going high means going low, and the secret way forward belongs to God alone. As a teacher, preacher, prophet, and evangelist who speaks around the globe, I'm committed to resurrecting the loveless soul of our churches and our culture, in Jesus' name. And if you're reading this book, I'm committed to helping you rediscover how to practice "the lost art of honor" and be restored to God's original, glory-filled design.

It's time to move beyond family-of-origin labels or mistreatment and learn the way of honor through examples from other times and places, unleashing peace, power, healing, and strength in yourself and others. As you read, God will open your eyes through some extraordinary personal stories I'll tell of spiritual identity. God will reveal secrets in ancient Jewish and Greek culture, plus in modern Asian culture, about honor, and he will bring new context to biblical truth through Christlike examples of honor for you to emulate.

As a word to those in my generation, I'm convinced that we are uniquely equipped to reclaim godly honor throughout the generations past, present, and future. We have the shared wisdom of our great-great-greats, the knowledge of our present age, and the prophecy/promise of a hope-filled, peaceful, abundant, and eternal life that starts today. It won't be easy. But it will be worth it. So let's tap into that collective generational wisdom and understanding of honor as a biblical imperative.

> For I know the thoughts that I think toward you, says the Lord, thoughts of peace and not of evil, to give you a future and a hope. (Jeremiah 29:11 NKJV)
>
> Mark the blameless man, and observe the upright; for the future of that man is peace. (Psalm 37:37 NKJV)
>
> "The thief does not come except to steal, and to kill, and to destroy. I have come that they may have life, and that they may have it more abundantly." (John 10:10 NKJV)
>
> For our light affliction, which is but for a moment, is working for us a far more exceeding and eternal weight of glory, while we do not look at the things which are seen, but at the things which are not seen. (2 Corinthians 4:17–18)

Honor: A Historical Perspective

Context is everything. And when it comes to honor, the only way we can see it in its right context is to understand where it originated from and how we have understood it (and misunderstood it) based on cultural norms. In biblical times, the ancient Greeks and Hebrews were not at all alike. Race, language, and cultures aside, the two groups didn't even *think* the same way. Greeks saw the world through the lens of abstract thoughts, while ancient Hebrews observed it through concrete thinking and feelings (which is why the Hebrew Old Testament was written in such a direct, straightforward manner).[1]

The vast Hebrew world of words opens our minds and our hearts to a deeper understanding of God's truly honorable character. Two Hebrew words are translated as honor, *hāḏār* and *kavod*. The former refers to honor as ornamentation, and the latter refers to the sheer weightiness of the honor bestowed. Rabbi Shlomo Wolbe gives us this background on *kavod*:

> The word "*Kavod*" is from the Hebrew root 'K.V.D.' (which means weighty or heavy). The diametric opposite is the word "*Klala*" (curse) which comes from the Hebrew root 'K.L.' (light). When I relate to someone with due seriousness I honor him, and if I treat him lightly it is as if I curse him.[2]

The takeaway? Honor is giving weight to the divine value you see in someone by demonstrating authentic respect or esteem for him or her. In many cases, this means promoting the person into a place of authority in your life.

Honor is giving weight to the divine value you see in someone by demonstrating authentic respect or esteem for him or her.

If we're honest, we will admit that we're quick to honor people when it comes to position, status, or wealth, but we're slow to honor when it comes to character. Honor is weighty, whether you choose to bestow it or not. Giving it manifests the weight of the glory of God; withholding it increases our weight of punishment (meaning that not giving proper honor where it is due may compound existing consequences for someone). Honoring God is also heavy in both solemnity and sacredness, and crowning or ornamenting him with glory and honor opens doors to heavy, *heavy* revelation.

Honor begets honor. Honor reaps honor. Honor manifests honor, when it originates with the Heart of Honor himself.

Here are the two Hebrew words for honor that appear in Scripture:

- הָדָר (n.), transliterated *hāḏār*. Appears thirty times in Scripture, meaning an ornament, honor, splendor, majesty, and glory.[3]
- כָּבוֹד (n.), transliterated *kāḇôḏ* (K.V.D, kâbôwd). Appears two hundred times in Scripture, meaning glory, honor, splendor, and abundance.[4]

While Hebrew brings the tangible "heavy revy" (heavy revelation) to the honor equation, Greek elevates the conversation entirely—to occasionally unhealthy levels. There are two Greek words for honor as well: *timê* and *doxa*. *Timê* refers to those who are worthy of glory, honor, praise, and worship in a very literal sense, often in a price context, while *doxa* refers to our opinions, judgments, or views of someone's worthiness of honor, good or bad.

- τιμή (n.), transliterated *timê*. Appears forty-three times in Scripture, meaning the literal value or worth of someone or something, often in a price context.[5]
- δόξα (n.), transliterated *doxa*. Appears one hundred sixty-eight times in Scripture, meaning the opinion, judgment, or view of one's worthiness of honor, good or bad.[6]

Language aside, there are two basic types of honor in the Greek language: ascribed honor and achieved honor. *Ascribed* honor is assumed or appointed by birthright and promotion. *Achieved* honor is earned through conquest, performance, actions, or behaviors.

But here's the interesting part: ancient Greeks viewed honor as a finite resource—meaning that if someone gained honor, someone else somewhere had to lose some.

Also, it's important to note that not all people in Greek culture could aspire to the same levels of honor; they were limited based on gender, race, birthright, and socioeconomic status. Slaves, for example, would almost never receive honor from someone above their station, even when their character warranted it.

Over the centuries, this widespread orphan spirit mentality has led people to compete within themselves and one another to try to gain a greater sense of self-worth, status, approval, and significance in life. The orphan spirit is a wandering spirit that leaves you empty while you're searching for fulfillment. Worse, this surface-level, works-based, performance-driven mindset has led many who found themselves in positions of perceived dishonor to take their own lives—as the most "honorable" thing to do.

When people's understanding of honor refuses to acknowledge basic human dignity and worth in this way, it's safe to say that our cultural perspectives on honor have been off for more than a generation or two. This may have been one of the reasons Jesus came in the first place.

1

What Is Honor?

"The Lord forbid that I should do this thing to my master, the Lord's anointed, to stretch out my hand against him, seeing he is the anointed of the Lord."

1 Samuel 24:6

No person was ever honored for what he received. Honor has been the reward for what he gave.

Calvin Coolidge

Entitled. Impulsive. Lazy.

If you're a millennial (born 1981–1996), or part of Gen Z (born 1997–2012), or even a rapidly rising member of Generation Alpha (born 2013–2025), chances are that you, like me, have heard these words spoken over you or your generation by parents, teachers, pastors, employers, and other authority figures.[7] As offensive as these complaints may be, I'm going to be straight with you: our elders have a point.

Now, don't get me wrong. The youth of our day are nothing short of exceptional. We know our worth. We balance work and rest. We dream big. We detest the status quo. But when it comes to honor? There, our elders are onto something. Honor *has* been lost on my generation (we millennials), but not for the reasons you might think. It's not because we are inherently rebellious. It's not because we are wired differently. It's not because we are self-absorbed, navel-gazing narcissists who can't see past our own noses. It's because when it comes to the lost art of honor, we've hardly ever seen it modeled authentically in the first place.

We are not the first ones to experience the deep and wide generational gap in mutual honor, respect, and understanding. Our parents once felt misunderstood by their elders too—as did our grandparents, great-grandparents, and all our great-great-greats. But I believe *our* generation carries a fresh and unique anointing to bridge that generational honor gap in Jesus' name—in a way previous generations never would or could have. Why? Because I dare say we are the first ones bold enough to break the mold. If we choose to receive and wield this honor anointing faithfully, I believe it will heal, unify, and unleash a once brutally broken, deeply divided body of believers, now poised and ready to take territory for the kingdom of God.

Unlearning and Relearning Honor

For something like honor to be lost begs several important questions:

- Did we ever have it in the first place?
- Do we know what it looks like, feels like, and sounds like?
- Would we know what to do with it if we saw it?
- Do we even know what we're trying to find?

Before we can learn what honor *is*, we need to start with what it's *not*. That's because most of us *think* we already know what honor is, but we don't. This critical process of unlearning the wrong definitions takes humility—a willingness to admit that you may not have always believed, thought, or acted rightly as it pertains to honor. I know I didn't.

Growing up in a Korean American home in Burbank, California, for me "honor" was a cultural imperative, rooted in centuries-old tradition. As a pastor's kid, I was also expected to be the very model of honor in our church and in society in order to bring honor to my father and mother. It's what good, God-honoring Korean kids do.

So I did as I was told. I bowed. I held my tongue. I saved *aaaall* the face. And it got me nowhere. Shortly after I was saved at a youth street revival at the age of eleven, I started to realize that my continued obedience, my selfless contributions, my God-given gifts, and even my voice were being largely ignored by my elders. Resentment grew in my heart, and rebellion festered in my spirit. Why was I expected to honor *them*, when they never celebrated, encouraged, or rewarded *me*? Why continue to show honor amid emotional abandonment and verbal abuse? Disgusted at the hypocrisy and unfairness of this so called honor, this well behaved Korean pastor's kid went wild, turning to alcohol, drugs, crime, and violence as my ways of sticking it to the man.

Yes, I still participated in the false honor I'd seen modeled. But I manipulated the narrative at every opportunity.

Yes, I still went to church. But I was noticeably drunk or high in every service (and *not* on the Holy Spirit).

Yes, I still lived under my parents' roof. But I transformed both our church and our home into drug-trafficking hot spots.

Yes, I still acknowledged my dad's authority. Primarily because I needed him to accompany me to juvenile court on the weekly for my transgressions.

Yes, I still held my tongue. I had no choice but to silently endure the abject condemnation from judges, juries, and would-be executioners.

But in time, I couldn't go through the motions of false honor anymore. When I realized "faking it" wasn't going to help me "make it," I stopped trying altogether. Dishonor burrowed deeply into my heart and spilled from my mouth, and I began cursing my father, my teachers, my elders, and other authorities in public with abandon. I willingly brought shame on my family and myself—which is pretty much the worst thing an Asian kid can do. That shame fueled my fury and brought me to a breaking point where I had no choice but to unlearn the false honor that had been modeled for me and relearn true honor in its appropriate kingdom context.

As my sins against my father and my God mounted, I found myself in deep, deep trouble. Dangerous men were after me. Officers had a warrant for my arrest. I was anxious, paranoid, desperate for something—anything—to save me from my self-made reality. For the first time since my childhood, I cried out to God for help.

God, if you're really real, get me out of this mess. Show me a way out—out of this house, this town, this country. Please, God! Get me out of here!

The morning after I cried out to God, my dad woke me up early with a question I never saw coming: "How would you like to go to Australia?"

Just days later, I was on a plane to the other side of the world, where I would rededicate my life to the Lord at a Youth With A Mission (YWAM) Discipleship Training School (DTS). "I sought the Lord, and He heard me, *and delivered me from all my fears*" (Psalm 34:4, emphasis added).

Throughout my journey away and back to God, I learned a few things about what honor is not:

- **Honor isn't forced.** When you honor someone because you have to, you may check a box, but you miss the point. True honor transcends expectation.
- **Honor isn't just about words.** You can speak, honoring someone with your mouth, but not mean a word of it. True honor flows from the heart.
- **Honor isn't tainted.** When you honor with ulterior motives (gaining power, money, influence, etc.), it's not pure. True honor isn't about personal gain.

By God's hand, I was moved with compassion to learn, unlearn, and relearn honor in its appropriate kingdom context within the first two decades of my life. It still blows my mind, but it serves a reminder that we're never too young (or too old, for that matter) to be chosen and anointed by God. We're on his timeline, which transcends time as we know it. This divine acceleration launched me straight out of high school rebellion into global itinerant ministry and almost immediately seated me alongside giants of the faith—fathers and mothers I never dreamed would one day know me by name and call me spiritual family.

Because I was willing to go low, to be humbled in the eyes of God and man, the Lord has raised me up to what I'm fully aware is a status and stature in the kingdom that most thirty-somethings long for. Before you think I'm teeing up for a humblebrag, know that I say all of this without an ounce of pretense. Because I know just how much it cost. For me, it cost my pride. For God, it cost his only begotten Son to *die* for that same pride. Christ's perfect sacrifice made up for my meager attempts and restored to me the joy of my salvation (Psalm 51:12).

While I wouldn't wish my experience of learning, unlearning, and relearning what honor is on anyone, I'm convinced that receiving it by grace and enduring it in faith has rebirthed and refined the man of God I am today—a man who not only lives by and is known for honor but who releases a spirit of honor everywhere he goes, in the magnificent name of Jesus Christ. A man who, by God's unfathomable grace, might even be brave enough, bold enough to call a rising generation of believers to embrace the lost art of honor and actually use our God-given keys to the kingdom.

As a man of God, I must know not only what honor is not but also what it is—what it means for those who experience its supernatural power.

- **Honor is healing.** It bridges the gap in relationships and rids your spirit of discord, dis-ease, and dysmorphia. *True honor redeems and restores.*
- **Honor is the key.** It solidifies your God-given identity, establishing value, dignity, purpose, and authority. *True honor is essential for success.*
- **Honor is supernatural.** It fills your whole being, flowing to you and through you as a stream of God's grace. *True honor is not of this world.*

Honor: A Biblical Mandate

Even after learning part of my story and taking a historical deep dive into the origins of honor, you may still have more questions than answers at this point. That's okay. Many see honor as old-fashioned, irrelevant, or even transactional—a "give it if you get it" kind of thing. This is why we must journey deeper into the biblical imperative of honor in the Word of God.

When Moses descended Mount Sinai in Exodus 19 and 20, and then again in chapter 34 with his face gleaming and the Ten Commandments in tow, the Israelites were scared to death of him (Exodus 34:29–35). He had just come face-to-face with the living God—and the aftermath of that encounter was nothing short of shocking to behold. Lightning flashes, trumpet sounds, smoking mountains. Not your everyday signs and wonders. The people literally trembled in Moses' presence, it was so weighty, mirroring the Lord's rich, thick, and heavy *kāḇôḏ* (19:16). They were about to get a dose of revelation no one saw coming—and out of the fullness of God's law, *honor* made the top Ten Commandments: "Honor your father and your mother, that your days may be long upon the land which the Lord your God is giving you" (20:12).

God's Word can be taken at face value here. It is good to honor our parents. But I believe this passage implies honor toward not only biological parents and legal guardian figures but elders and authority figures as well. We're to think highly of them—to honor, respect, and obey them. Peter reinforced this concept when he explained that we are to submit even to governmental authorities as "bondservants of God" (1 Peter 2:16; cf. vv. 13–17; 5:5–10).

This kingdom commandment is a strong declaration of honor as it *should be*—an extension of our oneness with God. Christ's own words point us to this reality: "At that day you will know that I am in My Father, and you in Me, and I in you" (John 14:20).

Note that Jesus doesn't say that at that day you will *be* one…he says that at that day you will *know* you are one. The problem is, we don't yet know we are one. Even if we know it in theory, chances are we don't quite believe it yet. Whenever "that day" is—today, perhaps?—you will come to understand what has always been true: giving blessing and honor and glory unto God brings blessing and glory and honor unto you and yours.

As finite beings, we miss the infinite magnitude of this reality. Every age, every culture, every generation, and every community has fallen short. Many Americans honor for the sake of personal gain, while many Koreans honor for the sake of legalism. Many Christians honor for the sake of favor exchange, while comparative religions honor for the sake of personal edification and enlightenment. We don't do this because we're inherently bad; we do it because it's what we've learned—what was modeled for us by the very elders we should be honoring. We, like the ancient Greeks, assume that honor must be calculated, earned, and transactionally reciprocated—demanded and even forced. We've bought into the legalistic lies that flattery and "fake it till you make it" honor will give us a spiritual, social, economic, and professional leg up against the competition in a perpetual "prosperity gospel" narrative.

Regardless of nationality, religious preferences, age, stage, and stature, we were created to emulate biblical honor as walking, talking, living, breathing image-bearers of our Creator God.

Yet regardless of nationality, religious preferences, age, stage, and stature, we were created to emulate biblical honor as walking, talking, living, breathing image-bearers of our Creator God. This is a clarion call to my generation—the Millennial Generation and beyond—to reclaim the lost art of honor and wield it God's way. (And if you're of an earlier generation, it's never too late for you to reclaim and wield honor either.) If not now, when? If not us, who? Why not *you*?

Honoring Immature Elders

If the concept of honoring your elders elicits an eye roll, you've likely encountered at least one or two of them who were, by all earthly standards, undeserving. The parent who abandoned you. The pastor who fell from grace. The officer of the law who abused his or her power. The list goes on.

Just ask David, the man after God's own heart. The shepherd boy achieved honor through his brave and mighty deeds in early life (hello, Goliath) and was ascribed honor by the prophet Samuel, who told him God had said he would be king.

But King Saul? *Not* a fan of David. He found him a little annoying at first, and then he grew wild with jealousy as David grew into a beloved war hero. Saul honored David with his mouth in public. He even gave David his daughter Michal in marriage. But it was out of obligation (*have* to), not from the heart (*want* to). Saul tolerated David's continual ascent into higher and higher places of honor until he just couldn't stand it anymore. Then David was unfairly persecuted, accused, tried, and sentenced to death by the jealous king.

David, though confused, deeply wounded, and publicly shamed by his beloved king, never faltered in honoring Saul and the office he carried. Even when presented with an opportunity to end the mad king's reign of terror, David spared Saul and chose to honor him—even though Saul didn't deserve it (1 Samuel 24:1–19; 26:1–9):

> David said furthermore, "As the Lord lives, the Lord shall strike him, or his day shall come to die, or he shall go out to battle and perish. The Lord forbid that I should stretch out my hand against the Lord's anointed. But please, take now the spear and the jug of water that are by his head, and let us go." (26:10–11)

David could have killed Saul quickly and quietly in that dark cave. Few would have blamed him, and most would have said it was justified out of self-defense or even as an act of war. But David knew honor was God's best—and until his own day came to fulfill Samuel's prophecy, he chose to honor the office of the king, no matter what. David was unquestionably the bigger man in this situation, and with a pure heart, he humbled himself before Saul and before God. And he didn't do it to endure abuse or accept death as inevitable, mind you—that's not what honor is. He did it to go low and honor his predecessor, even when it felt impossible. The result? Saul eventually fell on his own sword in shame, and God raised up David to be the next king.

David acted honorably, and Saul acted dishonorably. By earthly standards, David was worthy of honor, and Saul was not. But the harsh reality is that even the best of us is not *worthy* of honor. It's only Jesus Christ in us, the hope of glory, who makes us worthy. Deep down, David understood that humility is a powerful key to God's kingdom. After all, even David struggled to act honorably throughout his life and his reign as king. He committed murder and adultery, and he spent the rest of his life regretting it. But he continually allowed himself to be humbled by God. And God redeemed David's sin with a lineage that would one day lead to the Messiah's birth.

You won't honor others perfectly, nor will you live a perfect life worthy of honor. No human ever has—except one. And thanks to him, you can honor God's way: in the quietly courageous way of Jesus. By mining the gold in others, you'll uncover the treasure in your own spirit.

Honor: The Opportunity

In this day and age, we don't see many aspiring leaders honor the way David did. True honor has faded into the background of society and church alike. This is because generation after generation has demonstrated an increasingly diluted version of honor that, today, looks more like rebellion. Entire congregations split over worship preferences and carpet replacements, creating intentional distance and separation from one another. They refuse to honor the diversity within the divine DNA of the kingdom. Leadership becomes a conquest, with elders clinging desperately to the old way of things and aspiring leaders eager to usurp authority.

True honor has been lost because it hasn't been modeled. And to be fair, it hasn't been modeled for generations. We only know what we know when we know it, and that knowledge only becomes relevant wisdom when we choose to apply it in faith.

Honor looks like servanthood, no matter the cost. This is a tough concept for Americans to grasp, because most of us only seek to serve when it benefits us in some tangible way. But while the spiritual blessings that come with honor are very real, they don't always manifest in money, power, or fame in the natural world. That can make those of us in younger generations lose interest.

Typically, we see honor painstakingly structured as a movement from the bottom up, when it should rightfully be flowing from the top down as well. Elders should honor the younger generation by mining the gold in them and assuming authority over their potential, discipling and growing them in Christ Jesus. And the younger generation should honor their elders, not because they *have* to but because they *want* to acknowledge God's perfect legacy even in his imperfect vessels. Honor isn't deserved; honor is bestowed. And we must learn to honor the divine DNA in everyone.

Honor isn't deserved; honor is bestowed. And we must learn to honor the divine DNA in everyone.

But let's get real. Change can create chaos, and the longer we've been doing something, the more reluctant we will be to change it. If you consider yourself an elder by office, stature, or age, the important thing you can do as you read these pages is to demonstrate true honor to those you are called to shepherd and guide. The more familiar you are with what true honor means and how it is given and received in the kingdom, the more effectively you will demonstrate it. So keep reading! Whatever generation we belong to, we all have much to learn about honor.

If you are a millennial or younger—or if you are operating in a spiritual maturity that demonstrates breakthrough, acceleration, and growth—this book is written for you. God has put this message of honor on my heart for *our* generation for good reason. The world sees us as entitled, impulsive, and lazy. True or not, it is up to *us* to prove the world wrong by embracing honor in ways that bridge the gap between the generations—in ways our forefathers couldn't (or wouldn't). This is why I believe the younger generation is uniquely suited to reclaim the lost art of honor. Just because of our younger age and fewer experiences, we may have less baggage to shed in the process than our honorable elders.

Honor: The Secret to Success

My own journey with the Lord has been a whirlwind of glory. My fellow millennials see the hand of God on my life—favor, influence, followers, connections, authority, prosperity, signs and wonders—and they often ask me what my secret is. *Oh, if they only knew*, I often think.

Happening upon the status and stature required to fulfill my kingdom calling didn't come lightly. Most assume it must've been because of talent, skill, grit, and a willingness to build my platform brick by brick, like Nehemiah's wall. But that's not it at all. There are days when I wake up thousands of miles from my home in Southern California, invited to share the gospel with thousands of hungry souls, standing alongside giants of the faith. I know I don't deserve to be here. I'm only here because I went low.

After years of rebellion, I humbled myself before God, my family, my elders, and my peers—and God raised me up. Don't let the Gucci sunglasses fool you—I had to be willing to die to my old self completely for God to resurrect my wayward spirit and instill in me a God-honoring confidence that cultivates honor in my circles. As a senior pastor, an itinerant minister, and a child of God, the only honor and authority I carry is from the Lord.

While I didn't humble myself in order to be raised up, I'd be remiss if I didn't explain the tangible rewards that come with living a lifestyle of honor. I'm not dangling a carrot for you to bite. I'm just letting you know that it's honor—not striving, conquering, or knowledge—that gives you the keys to your kingdom inheritance in the natural world. Those of us who receive this inheritance now have authority to share it with others, which is why humility is the only way forward with honor. So let's discuss ten of the specific blessings honor unleashes in our lives.

1) Long Life

Exodus 20:12 not only expresses a biblical mandate for honoring your parents and elders; it also promises longevity when we walk in obedience to it. This can, in fact, manifest in literal long life—not just in years, but in overall quality of life. For example, when we read "It's better to live in a rickety shack than to share a castle with a crabby spouse!" (Proverbs 21:9 TPT), we know God cares about our relationships and our dwelling in addition to our health and longevity. Scripture proves humans lived hundreds of years in Bible days; Methuselah lived to be 969! But somewhere along the line, we partnered with death and embraced our own finality. Yet here's the good news: today, people are living decades longer than their fathers and forefathers, and some scientists believe future generations will live well into their 100s.[8] I am thrilled to acknowledge that this is at least partially because of advancements in medical science: science is of God and worthy of honor. But I also believe this biblical mandate of honor has a direct correlation to not only unreasonably long life in the natural world but also eternal life in the supernatural world. That long, abundant life Jesus died for you to have comes with great responsibility to demonstrate honor to future generations and train them in the way they should go.

2) A Good Name

When you walk in honor, you get a reputation for it, pure and simple. People who have received or even witnessed your love will have a great, godly perspective of who you are. Their confirmation of you releases not only the affirmation of God's truth over your life but also a testimony in society. Honor becomes a facet of your character and a representation of how the world views you, even when people don't align or agree with you completely. Consider for a moment: What do you want the world to say about you? What do you want your fellow leaders—both your elders and your peers—to think of you? While God's opinion of you is the first and only one that really matters, a good name and reputation are worth far more than riches of silver and gold (Proverbs 22:1). Walking in honor protects, preserves, and promotes this aspect of your kingdom inheritance.

3) Open Doors

Honor reinforces your good name and opens doors to people, places, and even realms that were previously inaccessible to you. Each person you encounter is a door that may in some way connect you to your God-defined destiny, so how you treat people really matters. Your behavior toward them can in fact determine access to heavenly resources—to the networks of people and even the regions of the earth you're called to reach for the kingdom. When you move in a spirit of honor, people will know you are trustworthy. That integrity will open doors in your life. People won't question who you are or whose you are; they will facilitate the opening of doors for you so you can enter easily. Honor attracts favor. Period. And when you walk in honor, you'll have access to people, places, and things most people will never access in their own strength. God, in his sovereignty, has predestined doors to open for you—and honor is the best way to participate willingly in becoming the man or woman of God you were created to be.

4) Wisdom

One of the top ways we show love is to listen. True honor seeks to understand rather than to be understood. It seeks not only to acquire knowledge but to apply it faithfully. Honor remembers that even as anointed vessels of grace, we are still jars of clay. When you walk in honor, you seek wisdom, which only comes through humility. When you honor what's in the lives of other people, you gain access to precious pearls of wisdom they have formed over the years, often through intense trial. They wouldn't insist you undergo those same trials and forge your own pearls. Far from it. They give wisdom freely and sacrificially, so your calling may be expedited and accelerated in this life. Whether pearl, gem, or gold, every person you encounter has something to teach you, something to impart to you to adorn your very own garland of grace with (Proverbs 1:8–9). Beauty. Adornment. Grace. These are your rewards.

5) Impartation

Without honor, you cannot receive from another person. The very act of receiving requires submission—opening your body and soul to others so they may pour blessings into you. When you dishonor someone in public or in your own heart, you close off your body and soul, and the blessing will ricochet off your dishonorable, hard-hearted armor. In order to walk out the fullness of God's blessings, you must understand that everything we have was once given to us—forged in the blood, sweat, and tears of those who came before us. Everything we have is an absolute privilege, part of a kingdom currency of honor. Impartation flows through this supernatural currency, which means that when you honor someone's sacrifice and the privilege it affords you, you will have access to greater benefits. These benefits can be entirely spiritual, but I can't tell you how many times I've seen such benefits manifest in access to airport lounges, hotel discounts, upgrades, and other tangible gifts that make it an even greater joy to do God's work. We laugh and call it favor, and it is. But it's also work—paying the high price of laying down your pride by honoring those who made a way for you. Favor isn't fair. Favor favors the ones who put in the work.

6) Connections

When you move in a spirit of honor, you share resources. What's mine is yours, and what's yours is mine. Because an honorable vessel can be trusted, connections and divine appointments are more easily made and given. The kingdom moves at the speed of relationships. And from a kingdom perspective, your network really *is* your net worth. When you move in honor, the Lord connects you with other honorable vessels, often outside your sphere of influence or place of residence. Honor enables you to break through natural boundary lines and other barbed-wire barriers to entry, so you can connect with people who carry different types of graces on their lives. Honor can take you anywhere—so long as you allow the Lord to chart your course.

7) Revelation

Honor is in itself a revelation of the Lord's character. He receives honor. He bestows honor. He is the author and originator of honor in all of creation. Only by intimacy with God will you receive more of his revelation of honor. Paul makes it clear in his letter to the church in Ephesus:

> Therefore I also, after I heard of your faith in the Lord Jesus and your love for all the saints, do not cease to give thanks for you, making mention of you in my prayers: that the God of our Lord Jesus Christ, the Father of glory, *may give to you the spirit of wisdom and revelation in the knowledge of Him*, the eyes of your understanding being enlightened; *that you may know what is the hope of His calling*, what are the riches of the glory of His inheritance in the saints, and what is the exceeding greatness of His power toward us who believe, according to the working of His mighty power which He worked in Christ when He raised Him from the dead and seated Him at His right hand in the heavenly places, far above all principality and power and might and dominion, and every name that is named, not only in this age but also in that which is to come. (Ephesians 1:15–21, emphasis added)

When you honor the Lord and his Word, he honors you. He will dish out the "heavy revy" to you, beloved child, because you are one who is ready to move from milk to meat. Honor moves God to share his secrets with you, facets of heaven that many may miss. Are you hungry for it?

8) Health

We know that honor brings longevity. But health and wholeness are key parts of that longevity. When you live at peace with God, he will cause even your enemies to be at peace with you (Proverbs 16:7). Honor will foster joyful, fulfilling relationships that will reflect honor on earth as it is in heaven. Even now, God prepares a table before you in the presence of your enemies so that you might invite them to come and dine with you on the rich flavors of his kingdom. This is *healthy*. It's countercultural, for sure, but it's healthy. What's more, honor doesn't just manifest in mental, emotional, and relational health; honor manifests in physical health as well. Dishonor breeds dis-ease. But honor overcomes it. It births children and families. It heals and restores. In fact, the divine positivity that comes with honor can actually bolster the immune system to rise up and fight cancer.[9] Honor can create a realm of protection over your mind, body, and spirit, enabling your fullest spiritual, psychological, and physiological potential.

9) Protection

Doing unto others as you'd have them do unto you isn't some new age karma (Matthew 7:12). You really do reap what you sow (Galatians 6:7–10). This eternal principle ensures that when you cast your bread on the waters, in due time it will return to you (Ecclesiastes 11:1). When you live in righteousness, you don't give the enemy a foothold. The armor of God is activated, protecting your soul and body in both the natural and spiritual realms. When you walk in honor, you walk in open heavens. You become aware of the legion of angels the Lord has sent on your behalf to aid and assist you. You're not alone; you're protected by your Sovereign. As an ambassador of grace in a foreign land, you carry sovereign rights and protection because you are a vessel of God's kingdom. You can live and walk victoriously wherever you go, knowing that God's honor—made manifest to you and through you—protects your name, health, wealth, and life and thwarts the attacks of the enemy. When you honor God, he will give you secret intel and expose any trap before you. This is what honor does. It keeps everything in the light. When you honor God, he will protect and defend you—even boast in you. You, my friend, are the apple of his eye. He delights in being your Defender against the ones who seek to dishonor, discredit, and destroy you. Honor unveils God himself—the Lord of angel armies.

10) Prosperity

Only when you honor yourself and others will you have the capacity to prosper. Prosperity isn't just about your finances, although that can be part of it. Prospering simply implies growth. Adopting a growth mindset means embracing change and becoming the best version of yourself—the "new you" Jesus paid the price for on the cross. Honor is the breath of life to your growth and prosperity. It's part of your divine DNA, which originates from the Holy Spirit living in you. That's why when you love others as you love yourself—when you honor others as you honor yourself—you will grow in dominion and authority daily as a king or queen in God's royal family. Take your seat of authority, for the Lord loves and honors you so much that Jesus gave his life so you can prosper and be like him today.

Honor: An Invitation

"If you love Me, keep My commandments" (John 14:15). These precious words from Jesus are some of the most sobering ever spoken. This authoritative command rhetorically insists that if we love Jesus, we will obey him—and that if we don't, we won't. Other inferences from the words of Christ include:

- If we love Jesus, we will love our enemies (Matthew 5:43–48)—and if we don't, we won't.
- If we love Jesus, we will live out the golden rule (7:12)—and if we don't, we won't.
- If we love Jesus, we will bestow honor freely (Romans 12:10)—and if we don't, we won't.

This begs a question, and your answer will echo throughout the generations: *Do you love him?* Your answer will determine whether you reclaim the lost art of honor and embrace the fullness of what God has for you—or not.

There is grace to cover you in this. And it's a good thing too, because you won't walk it out perfectly. But your calling is clear. Honor is our way forward, and humility is our path. It's a tough pill to swallow, but trust me, you're not going to want to miss out on this.

Honorable Reflections

What does true honor mean to you?

Have you ever felt dishonor in your church upbringing?

Have you ever received honor from an elder? If so, how did it make you feel?

Have you ever acted out on fleshly honor (have to) rather than honor from your heart (want to)?

2

Where'd the Honor Go?

Love one another with brotherly affection.
Outdo one another in showing honor.
ROMANS 12:10

It is in the character of very few men to honor without
envy a friend who has prospered.
AESCHYLUS

For honor to be lost on a generation, it must have, at some point, been in humankind's collective possession. Elder generations might assume they still have it—at least in part. And perhaps they do. But God's truth takes us all back to the last time we possessed honor in its fullness: in the beginning.

When God created Adam and Eve, he created them with honor as an intrinsic characteristic. As his image-bearers, they embodied godly honor by simply existing as a reflective representation of their Creator's glory. They weren't gods, but they were very much like God, formed and fashioned in his likeness (Genesis 1:27). They honored and obeyed God fully with joy and freedom—until the serpent asked a bold question that caused Eve to question for the first time whether God was honorable or withholding: "Now the serpent was more crafty than any other beast of the field that the Lord God had made. He said to the woman, "Did God actually say, 'You shall not eat of any tree in the garden'?" (3:1).

We all want to scream into the narrative at this point: "Yes, girl! Tell that serpent exactly what God said!" God really did tell Adam and Eve not to eat from the Tree of Knowledge of Good and Evil, and Eve knew it (2:17; 3:3). He didn't do it to hold out on them; he did it to protect them from seeking wisdom outside of himself—from relying on anyone or anything but him as their defining source of reality. Why? Because God alone was (and is) worthy of all honor.

As image-bearers, we will either bear God's image, which leads to righteousness, or bear another image of our own choosing, which leads to sin. When we rely on anything other than God to determine our identity, we will inevitably bear the graven image of whatever or whomever we turn to. In Eve's case, her attempt to be the lord of her own reality backfired. Big-time.

God really was, is, and will always be worthy of all our honor. Deep down, we know this is true—and my guess is that Eve knew it too. But honor without obedience is a false honor. When Eve entertained a lie and honored herself over God for a split second, the persona of sin wove itself deep into the fabric of our collective human experience. How many of us are guilty of identity atrocities like Eve's on the daily? None of us are immune. We've all fallen short. But thanks be to God, we've all been justified freely by God's unreasonable grace (Romans 3:21–26).

Honor without obedience is a false honor.

Honor wasn't lost on our generation. It was lost in Eden. We haven't seen anything quite like it since—except for the life and person of Jesus Christ. Honor himself chose humility, coming as a servant to redeem our lack of honor—our original sin—restoring us back into right relationship with our most honorable Creator. That redemption goes for you and me, for Eve and Adam, and even for the people we struggle to honor in this life. Because of Christ, we now have the capacity to rediscover and reclaim the lost art of honor by the power of the Holy Spirit living in us. It's what we image-bearers were always meant to do.

Systemic Honor

The honor we show in this day and age looks nothing like the honor we were bestowed with in the beginning. Since Eve lost her grasp on it in Eden, we've been trying to reclaim it in our own strength—resulting in a manufactured, systematic virtue system that actually breeds dishonor and division. We, like the ancient Greeks, still view honor as a finite resource—an expectations-laden social construct. We assume there's not enough honor to go around, so we withhold it—reserving it for those whom we deem truly *worthy* of honor. Like Eve, we choose to be lords of our own reality instead of image-bearers who only say and do what our heavenly Father says and does (John 5:19). This is true not only of our generation and our elders' generations, but *every* generation.

Our elders have never modeled honor perfectly. To be fair, it was never modeled perfectly for them either. Even our spiritual ancestors who sat with, talked with, and walked with Jesus were unable to emulate him perfectly when it came to honor. So why would we expect our elders to do so? Eve's original sin of self runs so deeply, so convincingly, that we struggle to see honor for what it really is on this side of the cross—a renewable kingdom resource. In fact, the Word of God insists that we are to "outdo one another in showing honor" (Romans 12:10). This will undoubtedly mean mining for gold, digging deep for something you can honor in everyone. Yes, *everyone.* Your parents. Your family. Your elders. Your civic leaders. Your teachers and preachers. Your law enforcement officers and uniformed officials. And yes, even *that person*—the one you can't (or won't) be bothered to muster up the honor for.

A spirit of honor (which we will talk more about in chapter 5) breaks off the spirit of entitlement that makes you believe you are wise in your own sight (v. 16). When you go low, meeting people right where they are instead of where you think they should be, you can find ways to honor the gold in them and acknowledge their potential as fellow image-bearers. When you can't find anything to honor in someone created in God's image, chances are you've made yourself the lord of your own reality.

Saul's End-Titlement

King Saul was, by earthly definition, worthy of honor in many ways. God handpicked him to be the first king of Israel, a role he grew into over time as he grew in his love for the Lord. For the most part, his subjects loved and obeyed him completely and without question. But in time, Saul's position of honor went to his head. He stopped honoring God and instead chose to be the lord of his own reality. First, he tried to usurp the role of a priest and offer a sacrifice to the Lord, which was blasphemy (1 Samuel 13). Then, he refused to follow God's very specific instructions on how to fulfill a prophecy of Moses by destroying the Amalekites with dignity (1 Samuel 15). Saul decided to do things his own way, humiliating, mutilating, and executing the fallen Amalekite king in front of the

Israelites. Despite the prophet Samuel's warnings, Saul refused to repent and dove deeper and deeper into dishonor—and God took his crown.

As satisfying as that conclusion might be, I encourage you to put yourself in Saul's shoes for a moment. You love God. You've been anointed as king of God's chosen people. You've got a stellar track record of honorable deeds. You've got a kingdom to run, and you can't be bothered with random rules and regs—anything that steals from your ultimate authority. What's more, you can't be bothered with *anyone* who steals from your ultimate authority. Especially some scrawny little shepherd boy turned giant killer.

Enter David, an out-of-nowhere up-and-comer who's anointed to be the *next* king of Israel—which, by the way, can only happen when *you* die (1 Samuel 16). You cringe when you see your protégé getting more honor than you. You try to give David honor where honor is due, but you also try to keep him in his place with tactics that escalate quickly into violence (1 Samuel 17–19). In desperation, you fight tooth and nail to maintain your own honor—what little bit of it you have left, anyway.

In our humanness, we can see things from Saul's perspective. Wayward as he was, the mad king had a point. Operating through a lens of scarcity and fear, Saul showed us what not to do when it comes to honor. But it's easy to see how he got to a point of desperation without the Lord guiding and directing his efforts.

Honor originated from the top down, from God into his creation. Our elders are meant to emulate that same honor, knowing it's far better to give than to receive. Despite Saul's manipulation, David continued to honor his king. He knew from a young age that he was anointed by God as Saul's replacement, but he never held that over Saul's head. He bestowed honor on Saul, refusing to take

Saul's life in self-defense—even as the mad king waged a war of dishonor against David and God (1 Samuel 24, 26). Saul's famous reign of dishonor came to an end without fanfare. He died by suicide, falling on his own sword during a battle with the Philistines where he lost his three sons (31:1–6). Saul didn't just lose his crown to dishonor—he lost his life and his family line.

As we dissect this biblical tragedy, you might be tempted to take the message at face value: *Don't be like Saul; be like David.* Yet David went on to make many of the same mistakes as his predecessor—because honor was never properly modeled for him by Saul, his elder. The deeper message is this: *Don't be like Saul. Don't be like David. Be like God.* Learn hard-won lessons from these kings, your ancestors, and you will be equipped and empowered to live out your kingly anointing by honoring the gold in everyone—especially the bright ones who will one day carry forth your legacy. Embrace Saul and David's royal anointing, redeemed in the shed blood of Jesus Christ, and you'll quickly learn that in the context of eternity, honor bestowed is far weightier and more beautiful than honor received.

Hard-Won Honor

After the rebellion of my adolescent years, I had many fences to mend. The most broken among them was my relationship with my father. Having to love me through my rebellion was undoubtedly a slap in his face, particularly from a Korean American cultural standpoint. My anger and vengefulness toward him were humiliating, but in that humbling season, he actually stepped up and became my father for the first time.

That may sound melodramatic, but let me assure you, I have no concrete early childhood memories of my father. When I try to reflect, it seems he was always about the ultra-busy business of ministry, pulled in a million directions at once—everywhere except home to his family, it seemed. Mom kept things running on her own until she couldn't take it anymore and left Dad on his own to full-on single-parent my older brother and me. He had no choice but to learn how to be present with us for the first time. The transition was *not* smooth. Dad felt like a stranger to me. I knew him not as "Dad," but as "the reason Mom left." It took years of him pursuing me—choosing to honor me, stand by me, and bail me out time and again—for me to finally understand his grace to me, his prodigal. When all else failed, love won.

Even though honor hadn't been appropriately modeled for me in childhood, I had no choice but to accept responsibility for the lack of honor I'd perpetuated far too long. Of course, I had no control over whether my dad would choose to now receive honor from me; I could only control my own heart, mind, and attitude in bestowing it with no strings attached.

Early into my conversion, it was difficult for my dad to believe I was truly a new creation. And who would blame him? The instantaneous, miraculous delivery I had experienced at YWAM was highly unusual in his circles, for sure. Seemingly overnight, I went from a life of drugs and violent crime to a life of passion and renewed purpose in the Lord. I was walking with giants of the faith. I was praying, prophesying, and evangelizing. I was stepping through every open door, totally sold-out for God. As my favor and influence grew, so did my dad's skepticism. He wanted to cling to the breakthrough I'd had, but he also worried that I'd lose everything with having too much freedom. Truth be told, Dad may have also been worried that my emerging ministry career might somehow steal honor from his own. I imagine he had thoughts like these:

Who does this kid think he is?
Correcting me *on* my *theology?*
How dare he?! He needs to get in line and learn a little humility.

For Dad, this meant doubling down on that age-old, patriarchal, authoritarian mindset—becoming a King Saul-esque authority over my David-like spirit. For me, this meant honoring Dad how he *needed* me to, even if it wasn't how he *wanted* me to. Namely, by speaking the truth in love to him, no matter the cost.

I honored Dad's house rules.
I *also* asked that he respect my personal space, my schedule, and my privacy.
I honored Dad with my mouth and my heart.
I *also* asked that he make an effort to express words of affirmation toward me.
I honored the Lord's anointing on Dad's life and ministry.
I *also* asked that he acknowledge the Lord's anointing on my *own* life and ministry.

It was different for both of us. Initially, he didn't like it. But unlike wayward Saul, my dad softened over time and made a genuine effort to honor me and my journey—mining the gold in me even when he didn't understand or agree. When elders would criticize my teaching, my style, my boldness, and the admittedly controversial kingdom company I often kept, Dad would defend me every time, calling out the new thing God was doing in and through me and redirecting their criticism to true discipleship. Dad didn't know exactly what I was hearing from the Lord, but he perceived it. He tasted and saw the sweet, juicy, highly appealing fruit of the Lord's blessing and honor on my life—and his *own* life to boot. When I moved out on my own, the healthy space allowed my relationship with my father to heal. I became my own man, free to leave, cleave to my heavenly Father, and achieve my full kingdom potential in my own way. It changed my relationship with my dad forever, and today, he remains one of my greatest champions.

This mutual honor was hard-won for both of us—but it was so worth it.

It takes both vulnerability and humility to find honor, especially within the family construct. Saul and David were not father and son in the natural meaning of the word, but their competitive dynamic rings true in modern-day families around the world. Children of all ages know that they're supposed to honor and obey their parents, but few parents remember that they're not to exasperate their children or provoke them to wrath (Ephesians 6:1–4). This truth requires both parents and children to own their part in the relationship and take responsibility for their actions, outdoing one another in honor.

Does this mean older children yielding to their parents' unrealistic demands? No.

Does this mean parents caving to their children's willful, dishonoring attitudes? No.

But it does require humility on both parts—a willingness to show respect no matter what. If God hadn't been faithful to humble me back to his heart, I never could have mustered the honor needed for the journey ahead. I had to learn to live in the dissonance of disapproval, demonstrating honor even in disagreement. *Especially* in disagreement.

Can you imagine a world where we applied this principle broadly? In our homes, in our churches, and in our communities? In academic pursuits, in corporate spiritual discernment, and in politics? If I have learned anything by embracing the lost art of honor with my family of origin, it's this: agreeing to disagree is only truly agreeable when honor is in the mix.

Heaven's Kiss of Honor

When you walk in a spirit of honor, you will be misunderstood. It's a painful reality, but it's one we must face head-on in order to practice this lost art.

Very early into my ministry career, I attended a revival conference. Travel, lodging, and tickets for myself and two of my spiritual daughters were a huge financial expense, but we were deeply hungry for more of God and thrilled at a chance to come together with other believers to worship him. We dove into the deep end the moment we set foot in the auditorium—worshiping freely, shouting joyfully, laughing fearlessly, dancing exuberantly—full-on *drunk* in the Holy Spirit. My heart could barely contain itself in the Lord's holy presence. "*Amen! Amen! Amen!*" My honor cry to the Lord rose above the crowd like incense into a growing cloud of glory.

I was so completely consumed by the presence of God that I was wholly unaware of my surroundings—which, unbeknownst to me, included a core group of elders who became increasingly perturbed with my displays of affection. Between my amens, they began correcting me: "Calm down. Be quiet! Show a little respect!"

But I couldn't stop rejoicing. Revival tasted so sweet on my tongue, and nothing on earth could stop me from bestowing honor and glory and blessing upon my Father. The corrections quickly rose in intensity, even to an instance of swearing in a worship service! Before I knew it, security people were escorting my spiritual daughters and me out of the auditorium into a second-floor overflow room. In hindsight, it was likely for our protection, but in the moment, it made me feel like a common criminal.

Being physically pulled away from the Lord's tangible glory left me feeling cold and exposed before my earthly authorities. Something was terribly wrong. Never in my life had I felt so targeted by elder believers—the ones I thought I had come to this conference to meet.

Over lunch, I processed my grief over the incident with my spiritual daughters. With full stomachs and heavy hearts, we surrendered our situation and started back toward the conference center in faith. On the way back, I spotted a woman (whom I recognized as one of the spiritual leaders of the conference) walking with her husband. She was a woman I would one day call "Mama Liz."

Knowing I had nothing left to lose, I introduced myself and humbly shared our experience through tears. As she drank it all in, I saw a righteous, godly, "mama-bear" anger rising in her. I felt seen, heard, and unconditionally loved by this powerful woman of God. She didn't take sides; she neither dishonored those who had shamed me nor overtly affirmed my abandoned worship style. Instead, she rose above the whole situation and rose up as my protector. She took me under her wing and invited my spiritual daughters and me to sit with her in the front row of the conference alongside all the speakers. This was certainly honor enough to make up for the earlier trauma, and I settled in with Mama Liz, drinking in the Lord's delight and favor. Being back in God's presence under the protection of Mama Liz was enough.

But God had more in store for me that day.

The conference keynote speaker, a globally recognized prophet named Shawn Bolz, singled me out from a crowd of thousands and asked me to stand so he could prophesy over me.

"Ben, God knows you love him out of purity," he began.

This acknowledgment was an immediate payback for the trauma I had faced that day. God was showing off his glory to me in front of a crowd of witnesses. As the prophetic words flowed like anointing oil, I knew the Lord was teaching me a profound lesson in honor. I had honored God before mankind in worship, willing to look like a fool and even be persecuted for doing so. So God honored me before everyone with a holy kiss from heaven, raising me up to sit with, talk with, and walk with giants of the faith—himself included! This required childlike faith from me, as the Lord suffered not this little child to be kept from coming to him (Matthew 19:14). He gave my spiritual family and me keys to the kingdom.

Honor Investments

When it comes to honor, what goes around comes back around. Jesus, Honor incarnate, made this concept abundantly clear when he walked the earth: "Therefore whoever confesses Me before men, him I will also confess before My Father who is in heaven. But whoever denies Me before men, him I will also deny before My Father who is in heaven" (Matthew 10:32–33).

Admittedly, the reciprocal promise of kingdom honor Jesus describes here doesn't always manifest immediately, as it did for me at that revival conference. Sometimes honor is an investment that takes years—a lifetime or longer—to yield a return of any kind. That's why we don't make honor investments in God and in people for a return. This tit-for-tat mindset is a product of false honor, and false honor is a product of a false gospel. Honor requires humility. Honor requires sacrifice. Honor requires selflessness—obedience unto death. We make honor investments because we're image-bearers of God, and we only say and do what he says and does. And when we continually walk in honor, we will continually taste and see the fruit of it.

The reciprocity of honor goes both ways. If honor begets honor, dishonor breeds more of the same. A man of God made this clear to Eli the priest, and God's words still ring true to us today: "For those who honor Me I will honor, and those who despise Me shall be lightly esteemed" (1 Samuel 2:30).

Honor is a weighty business, as we covered in chapter 1. To be "lightly esteemed" by God comes as a direct result of dishonoring him and dishonoring others. When we turn to anything or anyone besides our Maker, we will bear the image of what we behold. At times, we don't even realize we're doing it. Beyond possessions and wealth, we are prone to mistake a well-meaning religious spirit for God himself. We believe the lie that anything that doesn't seem clear through our unique God-shaped lenses *must* be of the enemy, including facets of the Father's character we have yet to experience. This limited perspective makes us think obedience is actually disobedience. Or makes us believe that what we first think is honorable is anything but.

None of us will walk out godly honor perfectly. Yet God, in his mercy, continues to honor us with his unmerited favor, his unfathomable grace. This grace is humbling. It *must* be humbling. Without this humbling, we won't be able to see beyond our pride to just how unworthy we are and how worthy he is. Only with this truth squarely in our sights can we ever be worthy of giving and receiving honor God's way—not because of anything we've done but because of what *he* has done—to us, in us, and through us. We would do well to remember this when we see believers of every age, stage, and station worshiping God in unique, diverse fashions. It takes a multi-reference, multi-preference, multicultural, and multigenerational approach to worship in order for us to give all honor and all glory to our multifaceted God.

Brotherly Honor

Of all the people we're called to love, family has the greatest propensity to hurt us. The intimacy, vulnerability, and close proximity that comes with doing life together (or apparent lack thereof) creates infinitely more opportunities for offense.

When Joseph, son of Jacob and Jacob's second wife, Rachel, was young, he hadn't yet fully grasped the concept of honor. The eleventh in a long line of brothers, Joseph was bestowed with the honor of birthright when his eldest brother, Reuben, the firstborn of Jacob's first wife, Leah, made himself unworthy (1 Chronicles 5:1). Jacob honored Joseph with a beautifully colorful coat as a symbol of this new birthright, an honor that stirred up intense jealousy in his older brothers.

To make matters worse, Joseph was clueless. In his immaturity, he was quick to let his brothers know just how honorable he really was. Tense as things already were, he fanned the flames of hatred by sharing his prophetic dreams:

> So he said to them, "Please hear this dream which I have dreamed: There we were, binding sheaves in the field. Then behold, my sheaf arose and also stood upright; and indeed your sheaves stood all around and bowed down to my sheaf." (Genesis 37:6–7)

Can you just picture his brothers rising to their feet, dusting off their hands, and cracking their knuckles, ready to pound their little brother? If they did, it didn't deter Joseph one bit. He dug himself deeper: "Look, I have dreamed another dream. And this time, the sun, the moon, and the eleven stars bowed down to me" (v. 9).

Joseph learned a powerful honor lesson that day: *Read the room.* Sometimes a word from the Lord is meant to be shared with everyone—and sometimes his whispers of delight are meant as precious gifts just for you. Joseph didn't pause to think about how his dreams, true as they were, might make his brothers feel. And unfortunately, it consumed their hearts with a jealous rage so fierce that they sold him into slavery and told their father he had been killed.

When or if you choose to share the honor bestowed on you, doing so in humility is critically important. When honor is bestowed, it's important to remain sensitive to those caught in a scarcity-minded, orphan spirit. They may be impacted by the honor you receive.

But even in our stumbles, God always has a plan. Joseph was sold to Potiphar, the honorable captain of the guard under Pharaoh. Not a bad gig for a slave. God was with Joseph, and Joseph was highly esteemed in Potiphar's household, which was unusual for someone of his station. But when he honorably refused to lay with his master's wife, a conspiracy against him sent Joseph to prison (Genesis 39).

Still, even in our setbacks, God always has a plan. Joseph found favor in the eyes of the jailkeeper and was permitted to have authority over the prisoners. He began interpreting dreams and was eventually called from his cell to interpret the dreams of Pharaoh himself! Joseph was pardoned and seated in a place of high honor as Pharaoh's right-hand man, ruling over all Egypt (Genesis 41).

And even in our successes, God always has a plan. Joseph led Egypt to prosper through years of famine. The country was so prosperous that other tribes would visit the land to buy grain. Joseph's father sent his brothers to Egypt to do the same. In a dramatic climax, Joseph stood clothed in honor before his brothers, whose faces were in the dirt as they bowed before him—just like in his dream. He was in such a high place of honor, they didn't even recognize him.

Thankfully, our friend Joseph had gained a healthy dose of humility by this point. He took a moment to compose himself, allowed the Lord to fill him with grace, and revealed his true identity. He kissed, blessed, and richly provided for the brothers who, even through an act of betrayal, had fulfilled God's will to preserve not only Joseph's life but also theirs. This is how image-bearers of God reveal his glory—honoring others by being kindly affectionate in brotherly love, even when their elders act less than honorably. As Joseph told his brothers, "But as for you, you meant evil against me; but God meant it for good, in order to bring it about as it is this day, to save many people alive. Now therefore, do not be afraid; I will provide for you and your little ones" (50:20–21).

Rediscovering Honor

If honor is a lost art, where'd it go? This honest question unearths a powerful truth in our collective perspective as God's image-bearers. Honor isn't lost. The art of *practicing* it is.

Honor himself has set up residence in our hearts, and nothing can separate us from his love (Romans 8:35–39). He always has been, and he always will be, right within our grasp. We're the ones who turned away. We've collectively turned our backs on Honor himself, compounding and perpetuating our deception regarding honor's whereabouts from generation to generation. We've become our own little gods—lords of our own realities—scraping and biting for scraps of false, earthly honor in order to maintain our safety, security, and significance.

Honor was and is and always will be in our collective possession. It's a powerful kingdom tool, but we often simply refuse to use it. Why? Pride. Friend, we were made to reflect more than this.

Honor was and is and always will be in our collective possession. It's a powerful kingdom tool, but we often simply refuse to use it.

Walking in true honor isn't easy. It's countercultural, wholly representative of the upside-down kingdom of our heavenly Father. As you choose to walk in honor, it will feel more natural to you in time—but true honor is never easy. Honor will cost you something, as does any worthwhile investment.

The apostle Paul wasn't one of Jesus' twelve disciples. Like us, Paul (who was also, ironically, called "Saul") didn't even know Christ before the crucifixion. And yet, Paul was arguably the most powerfully persuasive witness to Christ's resurrection in all of Scripture (Acts 9:1–19; 22:6–16; 26:12–23). Paul's letters discuss the topic of honor more than any other book in Scripture, challenging our assumptions on what it is, where it comes from, and why it is important. Honor is direct—never passive-aggressive, calling out tyranny and calling the body of Christ to repentance.

Honor can be confrontational—especially when it comes to keeping God at the center of our collective reality. To religious legalists, honor can seem rebellious, but it is actually reformative and necessary. When you fear God more than you fear people, you're more willing to assume risks and even disappoint people without compromise. Honor looks, acts, and feels like Jesus.

For our generation to reclaim the lost art of honor, we must learn to respect, value, and honor wisdom—while also discerning whether a particular bit of wisdom is for us or not. And when it's not? We must learn to show honor all the more in disagreement. Not because we have to. Not because we should. But because we're image-bearers—and it's what we do.

Honorable Reflections

Was there a time when you had to dig deep to truly honor somebody?

Is true honor easy to display? Why or why not?

What has honoring God cost you?

How can you honorably disagree with your elders?

3

A Culture of Honor

"What is man, that You are mindful of him, or the son of man, that you care for him? You made him for a little while lower than the angels; you have crowned him with glory and honor, putting everything in subjection under his feet."

HEBREWS 2:6–8

In a culture of honor, leaders lead with honor by courageously treating people according to the names God gives them and not according to the aliases they receive from people.

DANNY SILK

Reclaiming the lost art of honor in our day will take more than knowledge and understanding. It will take humility, wisdom, and tons of trial and error, especially in the context of Christ-centered community. Church culture is everything: after all, it's a collective manifestation of divine awareness. Fostering a culture of honor will infuse honor into the customs, arts, social institutions, and achievements of the people you love and lead. Culture on the outside is a manifestation of who we are on the inside—who we are in secret. It's not just what we believe or what we do; it's who we are.

Honor in culture embraces identity and purpose, seeking to drive destiny and outcomes for individuals and groups alike. And a culture of honor is the culture of the kingdom of God, manifest on earth as it is in heaven.

Practicing the lost art of honor looks like something—or more appropriately, like someone. Honor looks like Love himself.

Scripture tells us a great deal about love, and Paul's first letter to the church in Corinth makes love's true nature abundantly clear. In 1 Corinthians 13:4–8, Paul tells us these things about love:

- Love suffers long and is kind.
- Love does not envy; love does not parade itself, is not puffed up.
- Love does not behave rudely, does not seek its own, is not provoked, thinks no evil.
- Love does not rejoice in iniquity, but rejoices in the truth.
- Love bears all things, believes all things, hopes all things, endures all things.
- Love never fails.[10]

Each poetic stanza of this passage calls believers to a higher standard of love for one another, establishing the Father's heart for authentic, godly relationships. We Christians will be known by our love put on display within a *culture* of honor. If Paul were to put these ideas to paper, I imagine it would read something like this:

Honor is selfless and true.

> Honor does not force; honor does not corrupt, is not fake.
>
> Honor gives weight, gives value; it respects and esteems.
>
> Honor seeks not to be earned, but is lovingly bestowed.
>
> Honor flows from the heart, transcends expectation, gives gracefully, exists peacefully.
>
> Honor is love in action.

Modern mainstream conversations about culture aren't about churches or communities; they are about companies and organizations. Trailblazing entrepreneurial leaders like Elon Musk, Gary Vaynerchuk, and Patrick Bet-David are transforming life as we know it by building healthier, more empathetic corporate cultures. Balancing their intellectual quotient (IQ) with their emotional quotient (EQ) in leadership styles and defined cultural expectations allows them to mobilize, equip, and empower their people to achieve more together. Now, I will never treat the body of Christ like a business. But I do honor the divine DNA in these forward-thinking leaders, and I believe the church could learn a great deal about healthy culture-building by observing the modern day Cyruses in our midst.

For better or for worse, strong leadership directly influences culture. When leaders walk in honor, honor manifests in the people. When they don't, it doesn't. And the modern workforce won't stand for that any longer. New research shows that nine out of ten millennials will take a pay cut to work for a company with a culture that shares the same mission and values as they do.[11] Some naysayers might call this behavior foolishness or even narcissism, but I call it profound wisdom. Integrity demands we do work that aligns with our calling. Even if you don't work in a ministry context, your work, or vocation, is a modern-day mission field where the divine calling on your life can be clarified and mobilized.

Interestingly, though, no matter how great the company culture, a person's direct supervisor has the greatest impact on overall job satisfaction and loyalty.[12] If leaders are intellectually and emotionally healthy, they will naturally bestow transferable honor onto their team members in the overflow. If they are not, they will breed dishonor in their subordinates, creating a generational culture gap in the company that preys on the weak, exploits the strong, and devalues human creativity and work ethic. Burnout rages, conflict and abuse erupt, and ultimately, breaches in working relationships are unavoidable.

The application of these business realities in kingdom cultures has the potential to change the church forever when it comes to honor. We can then articulate our mission, values, and community behaviors with clarity and boldness—and we will attract people and prophets who can help us mobilize a move of God.

Building a culture of honor at work, at church, or at home is no small task. Sustaining honor within that culture proves an even greater challenge. Like love, honor can be messy in a community context, predominantly because of unarticulated, unmet, or unreasonable expectations. In bringing together a diverse group of image-bearers—each one reflecting a unique facet of the Father's character—we can experience a revelation of our Creator's true character, which is shown only in the beauty of our oneness. Celebrating diversity and uniting under a set of agreed-upon core values, we can take our rightful place as the church—the bride—ready for her heavenly Groom.

Seven Core Values of Honor

Where two or more are gathered, there's bound to be disagreement at some point. Competing priorities. Unique preferences. Varied experiences and perspectives. And let's not forget pride. Acknowledging and even creating room for healthy conflict, disagreement, and debate are essential to practicing the art of honor in community. But the secret to building a culture of honor goes deeper than mere practice. A culture of honor must originate from the very foundation of a community with a unified, agreed-upon set of core values that honor God and one another no matter what.

A culture of honor must originate from the very foundation of a community with a unified, agreed-upon set of core values that honor God and one another no matter what.

I humbly present seven core values of honor—values that have shaped cultures of honor in my own Christ-centered communities in Southern California, across the nation, and around the world. These seven core values are *championing others*, *making space*, *being unoffendable*, *gratitude always*, *freedom to fail*, *love first*, and *unshakable loyalty*. Let's explore each of these a little more closely.

1) Championing Others

Gathering in Jesus' name is one thing, and making commitments to disciple is another. But what about empowering others? What about believing the best in them and giving them opportunities to hone their gifts and step into their calling? This is something else entirely. The word *champion* has a variety of meanings. As a noun, it can be someone who wins or shows marked superiority, but it can also be someone who advocates and defends—a warrior who literally and/or figuratively does battle for another's rights and/or honor.[13] What's more, as a transitive verb, to *champion* describes not only our roles, but also our actions and responsibilities within a culture of honor. We are champions who champion—because of what our collective Champion, Jesus Christ, has done for us.

> Therefore, since we are surrounded by such a huge crowd of witnesses to the life of faith, let us strip off every weight that slows us down, especially the sin that so easily trips us up. And let us run with endurance the race God has set before us. We do this by keeping our eyes on *Jesus, the champion* who initiates and perfects our faith. (Hebrews 12:1–2 NLT, emphasis added)

2) Making Space

It takes years to create sustainable culture. In some cases, it takes decades and even centuries. So it's no wonder leaders are protective of their flocks, their traditions, and their agreed-upon ways of life. Along with this steadfastness, a true culture of honor recognizes that God is still speaking, and that when he does so through even the most unlikely of vessels, we had better listen. When our old ways of doing things stunt growth, progress, and development, we're no longer honoring the legacy that has been built; we're clinging to it in desperation, instead of clinging to Jesus.

A culture of honor creates intentional space for new ideas, new people, and new ways of doing things in a biblical context. That means discipleship techniques like teaching, correction, and even rebuke—massaged in with time, relationship, and sensitivity—must be laced with copious amounts of grace and love.

> "Do not remember the former things, nor consider the things of old. Behold, I will do a new thing, now it shall spring forth; shall you not know it? I will even make a road in the wilderness and rivers in the desert." (Isaiah 43:18–19 NKJV)

3) Being Unoffendable

Because conflict is an expected and necessary component of healthy community, those of us loving and leading within a community must walk in a level of honor that totally transcends offense. Being unoffendable is impossible in your own strength, which is why we need a supernatural impartation of grace that transcends earthly logic. Quickly turning the other cheek. Forgiving and forgetting, again and again. Believing the best in people instead of succumbing to skepticism and cynicism. Whether or not the offenders in your circles are repentant, honoring them anyway allows you to walk in purity before God, bearing no grudges. Yes, boundaries may be necessary. All healthy relationships have them. Yes, correction may be warranted. All children of God need it. But being unoffendable means not sinning in your anger. It means pursuing restoration and reconciliation *relentlessly.*

> "Be angry, and do not sin": do not let the sun go down on your wrath, nor give place to the devil. (Ephesians 4:26–27)

4) Gratitude Always

Keeping a culture of honor requires an uncompromising attitude of gratitude, both in joy and in sorrow. In abundance and in scarcity. In new beginnings and in necessary endings. In life and in death. In all things, being thankful to God for his good gifts, knowing that he alone is more than enough. This mindset goes far beyond mindfulness to a level of connection and an awareness of being one with your Creator God. It requires intense obedience—focusing on the finished work of the cross instead of your very real surroundings. As you walk with others through the trials of this life, keeping a spirit of celebration and thanksgiving might look like rejoicing with those who rejoice, weeping with those who weep, and being of the same mind that is in our Lord Jesus Christ (Romans 12:15–16; Philippians 2:5–11). It means celebrating vulnerability. It means offering prayers of thanksgiving, even in times of deep loss and strife. It means embracing true contentment regardless of circumstance and remembering that God is always working all things for our good and his glory (Romans 8:28). Wanting for nothing. Needing for nothing. Believing in faith for everything, because Jesus is truly enough. As Paul put it,

> Not that I speak in regard to need, for I have learned in whatever state I am, to be content: I know how to be abased, and I know how to abound. Everywhere and in all things I have learned both to be full and to be hungry, both to abound and to suffer need. I can do all things through Christ who strengthens me. (Philippians 4:11–13)

5) Freedom to Fail

We talk a great deal in church circles about religious freedom—the freedom to act, think, and worship in ways that honor God, even when others don't agree with our methods. While I think we have plenty of religious freedom—perhaps too much at times to be healthy, if I'm completely honest—there is one area where I believe we as the church could collectively loosen our grip a little: failure. For people to authentically experience God and pursue growth in him, they must be willing and able to fail. As finite beings trying to understand an infinite God, we are bound to make mistakes. Freedom to fail gives people permission to walk out an imperfect existence alongside a perfect God who can and will redeem it all. Make no mistake: you are holy and blameless in God's eyes (Colossians 1:22). But we are all works in progress, continually aligning with the truth of our holiness—a reality that Jesus died for. A culture of honor gives people permission to fail—to be in process, free of judgment, with no one trying to control outcomes. When we honor people in failure, we allow them to fail forward and rise up stronger and wiser than they once were.

> For a righteous man may fall seven times and rise again, but the wicked shall fall by calamity. (Proverbs 24:16 NKJV)

6) Love First

Love is the most accurate measure of kingdom integrity within a culture of honor. And it looks like something—or, more appropriately, like someone. Love looks like being the first to serve. The first to sow. The first to reach out in selflessness, even at great inconvenience. Love looks like doing the hard things first—not to earn some kind of Sunday school gold star, but simply because they're the right things to do. Love looks like being the first one through the door, ready to go above and beyond even when no one is looking. *Especially then.* Loving first often means putting yourself last, which is admittedly countercultural in an era of self-love. But in this upside-down kingdom realm, the last will be first, and those who go low will rise (Matthew 20:16; James 4:10). As image-bearers, we can't help but love, because he loved us first.

> There is no fear in love; but perfect love casts out fear, because fear involves torment. But he who fears has not been made perfect in love. We love Him because He first loved us. (1 John 4:18–19)

7) Unshakable Loyalty

Honor and slander cannot coexist. We're quick to forget this in Christian community, where even well-meaning prayer-chain submissions can turn into gossip, secrecy, distrust, and betrayal. Image-bearers are called to highly esteem their fellow image-bearers—always giving them the benefit of the doubt. To do otherwise can lead one into demonic witchcraft, which is rebellion and going against God's truth concerning his beloved. Are we anti-Christ by our loose lips or pro-Christ by our love and graceful words? Real honor protects others from misunderstanding and assumes the best even in the worst circumstances, knowing that whatever truth God brings into the light, he will be faithful to redeem it. Honor doesn't entertain lies; it seeks truth and follows church discipline to the letter, as Jesus taught in Matthew 18:15–19. When issues of sin and offense are addressed face-to-face instead of in the shadows, truth will be revealed and progress can be made. Friend, I implore you, don't even be curious about gossip against someone you honor. That person is innocent until proven guilty—and even then, honor is the only way forward. Practically speaking, hating the sin and loving the sinner means mining pure gold from within a jar of clay. Your good Father will go mama-bear on anyone who speaks falsely against his kids, even when his children are in the wrong. Do only as your Father does in defending honor against the odds.

> Let no corrupt word proceed out of your mouth, but what is good for necessary edification, that it may impart grace to the hearers. (Ephesians 4:29 NKJV)

Seven Core Values of Honor

1. Championing others
2. Making space
3. Being unoffendable
4. Gratitude always
5. Freedom to fail
6. Love first
7. Unshakable loyalty

Guilty Until Proven Innocent

Defining and aligning under a unified, agreed-upon set of core values was a hard-won victory for my Christ-centered communities—one that called my own honor into question. Years ago, I faced some false but fierce allegations about my conduct and character as a pastor. People I loved, esteemed, trusted, and ministered alongside threw me under the proverbial bus without so much as a phone call. They refused to protect, defend, or even consider my innocence. As they came maliciously against me with no biblical protocol, gossip spread, doors were closed, and events were canceled.

Having my honor called into question put such a strain on my good name and reputation that I engaged our ministry board and legal counsel to perform an intense three-month investigation into these allegations. I laid my life bare before the elders and my God and pleaded the words of the psalmist: "Search me, O God, and know my heart; try me, and know my anxieties; and see if there is any wicked way in me, and lead me in the way everlasting" (Psalm 139:23–24).

The result? There was not even a *shadow* of truth to the allegations. And yet, even after proof of my innocence, I spent years doing damage control. A small group of leaders repented and honored me once again, and I welcomed them back into the fold, forgiving and forgetting. But most of my accusers preferred to stay in the dark, perpetuating suspicion and lies with zero proof. These individuals continued to try to defame my name and destroy my ministry, acting as image-bearers of the lie they were beholding—until I took legal action. Today, I walk free in God's truth, knowing that Jesus fought for my honor, and that when he did, one by one all my accusers walked away.

Painful as it was to be misunderstood, this experience uniquely equipped me to walk with other brothers and sisters, sons and daughters of the faith who are falsely accused—believing them and believing *in* them all the way, defending their honor unequivocally. No wisdom is wasted when it comes to honor.

Innocent Until Proven Guilty

Here's the hard part about existing within a culture of honor: sometimes the rumors are true, at least in part. And when they are? Honor becomes arguably even *more* important.

Case in point: When a woman was caught in the act of adultery in John 8 (some argue it was Mary Magdalene), we see Jesus' gospel of honor on full display. Sketchy as "catching her in the act" of adultery may have been, Scripture implies that this woman knew she was guilty—even if entrapment and spiritual manipulation had played a part in her defamation. Jesus knew she was guilty too. But instead of choosing to fan the flames of cultural offense by checking a religious box, he chose to honor and protect her good name by identifying the hypocrisy of her accusers. Instead of pointing his finger in condemnation, he went down low and used it to draw a figurative line in the sand:

> But Jesus stooped down and wrote on the ground with His finger, as though He did not hear.
>
> So when they continued asking Him, He raised Himself up and said to them, "He who is without sin among you, let him throw a stone at her first." And again He stooped down and wrote on the ground. Then those who heard it, being convicted by their conscience, went out one by one, beginning with the oldest even to the last. And Jesus was left alone, and the woman standing in the midst. (John 8:7–9 NKJV)

No one knows exactly what Jesus wrote in the sand that day. Some speculate that he wrote a list of names; others suspect a list of egregious offenses committed by the crowd. Part of me wonders if he simply exposed the Pharisees' plot to discredit him. Whatever he wrote, it struck a chord of conviction that encouraged the onlookers to worry about the log in their own eye instead (Matthew 7:3–5). Starting with the elders, the most likely coconspirators, they all threw down their stones and walked away. As this poor woman, broken and laid bare before her peers, stood awaiting certain death for her transgressions, her Messiah bestowed honor upon her that transformed her life forever:

> When Jesus had raised Himself up and saw no one but the woman, He said to her, "Woman, where are those accusers of yours? Has no one condemned you?"
>
> She said, "No one, Lord."
>
> And Jesus said to her, "Neither do I condemn you; go and sin no more." (John 8:10–11)

Sometimes the rumors are true. But even when they are, we need to be willing to collectively embrace the image-bearer inside the enemy. Now, don't hear what I'm not saying. Sin in our communities must be addressed with conviction and compassion. But grace is, by definition, "unmerited favor." Honoring someone even in his or her failures makes room for God to go low, as Jesus did for the adulterous woman, and raise the person up again in him. Jesus' gospel of honor shattered the religious and political systems of the day and tore down a prevailing hierarchy of self-righteousness.

I'll be straight with you: Doing honor the right way, God's way, can backfire in the natural world. Big-time. Entitled sinners will inevitably misuse grace as an excuse to sin. They will misrepresent honor as an opportunity to forward their agenda. And there is nothing you can do to control it in your own strength. Sometimes you'll need to lean in hard and keep on pressing. Sometimes you'll need to dust off your sandals and move on. Don't waste your time and your pearls, but don't get too attached to them either. Go all in with honor, believing the best even when you don't know or understand the outcome. In all things, let the mind of Christ be in you, bestowing honor for the sake of Honor himself. In doing so, you will become a conduit of supernatural grace that brings honor to the brethren, to yourself, and to the God who calls you low to raise you up.

The Honor Equation

When it comes to a culture of honor, we can be tempted simply to "break even" in purely transactional exchanges. For some of us, even those of us who hate math, honor becomes an equation we try to solve. We pour into others—only to be filled ourselves. We lift others up—as long as it elevates our own reputation. And we empower others' success—when their success fuels our own agenda. If we're honest, we'll admit that we "give it to get it" far more than we should.

What's more, when we don't receive honor as we think we deserve to, we are unlikely to give it as we should, perpetuating the lie that justice always looks like balanced scales. "Should-ing" aside, we're called to "outdo one another" in showing honor (Romans 12:9–16). Going above and beyond to show honor goes far beyond saving face. It's risky. It's sacrificial. And from a purely human standpoint, it *does not compute.*

Solving for honor is impossible—because the honor equation isn't really an equation at all. Honor multiplies faster than calculators can crunch. Honor is not a prerequisite for honor, nor is honor a tool to be wielded for self-righteousness. Honor is a variable that hangs patiently, waiting to be bestowed so it can create a ricochet effect of honor upon honor upon honor in our communities. Honor is not a goal; it is the source—a catalyst for true kingdom relationships within a culture of honor. Honor is love in action, so in a culture of honor, love wins.

Fostering an Authentic Culture of Honor

In today's divisive and dismissive culture, false honor is an idol the church simply can't afford to entertain. Positions, platforms, and the powers that be have their place, but when we honor people based on these factors alone, we miss the point. A true culture of honor does two important things: (1) it emulates the life of Jesus, and (2) it empowers the no-names. Jesus never failed to love the ones right in front of him—giving the overlooked ones a look and passing on those in high position—unless, of course, he thought the high ones might leave it behind to follow him. You didn't need to be a millionaire donor to get Jesus' time. In fact, he saw and named the value in the least of these, the ones nobody expected to do anything exceptional.

In discipling conversations about honor culture, I get a host of coulda, shoulda, woulda excuses. Here are a few of the most pervasive:

> *I would show honor, but honor is never given to me.*
>
> *I know I should act honorably, but what's in it for me?*
>
> *I would love to be part of a culture of honor—if I could only find one.*

Friend, enough! Stop trying to solve for an honor equation that doesn't exist. Bestow honor with no strings attached. Start with a clean slate and uncompromisingly walk in honor. And if you can't find the culture of honor you want to see? Try being it instead.

And if you can't find the culture of honor you want to see? Try being it instead.

In case you hadn't noticed, even amid unprecedented revival, there's a mass exodus happening in the Christian church.[14] People are leaving in droves—not because they're giving up on Jesus, but because of the same centuries-old hypocrisy he spoke so vehemently against. Organized religion has been tainted with dishonor, and emerging generations of believers won't stand for it. Herein lies the opportunity for the Millennial Generation and younger: honor doesn't just beget honor; honor *attracts* honor. And the Jesus in you will attract the Jesus in the people around you—even if the shape of your culture looks different than it ever has before. It'll look less like power, influence, and wealth and more like humility, intimacy, and generosity. It'll look less like a stage and more like a secret place. It'll look less like you and me and more like Jesus.

If, with clean hands and a pure heart, you really want to walk alongside giants of the faith, *emulate* the Christlike honor you see them bestow on others—especially to the least of these. And when you do? You'll find yourself in angelic company for all your days.

Honorable Reflections

What is your first memory of extravagant love and honor?

How do honor and loyalty go hand in hand?

If Jesus honored the least of these, what does that mean for you?

In your opinion, what constitutes a culture of honor?

4

Honor: Heaven's Currency

Render therefore to all their due: taxes to whom taxes are due, customs to whom customs, fear to whom fear, honor to whom honor.

ROMANS 13:7 NKJV

When you choose to honor, it allows you to purchase and pass through places—both in the physical and spiritual realms—that would otherwise be closed off.

RABBI CURT LANDRY

My colors are clear. For my generation or anyone to reclaim the lost art of honor, we must be willing to go beyond box-checking transactions. We must invest in honor futures as freely as Elon Musk invests millions in pocket change in Bitcoin. You can't buy or sell in the kingdom of heaven without playing in the market of peace.

But let's elevate the honor conversation a step further. Honor isn't a standard buy-or-sell currency, at least not in the natural world. But from a supernatural kingdom perspective, honor is legal tender—worth far more than gold, the US dollar, or any other fiat money. Honor is valuable currency in the economy of heaven. Without recognizing and participating in this currency exchange, we won't be able to go deeper with God, taking on his supernatural mantle of honor in a way that dramatically impacts our world.

God resists the proud and rewards the humble. Not just with extra room in our mansion in glory one day, but in the here and now. The return on investment for honor bestowed produces tangible earthly outcomes. Purpose. Favor. Open doors. Provision. Resources. Connections. We are destined to receive these holy dividends, because we are meant to walk in honor as image-bearers of God.

Now, honor as currency isn't to be given or taken lightly, because honor is no earthly currency. It is precious, weighty, and infinitely valuable. It's not meant to be usurped or manipulated but rather sown and reaped in faith. It should never be rooted in selfishness or ambition but should always consider and empower others. Even when you go low, move in purity, and do your best to honor the divine DNA in all, people *will* fail you—but God never will. Your risks and sacrifices in this world are noticed and appreciated by your Father in heaven. God will pay you back—or better yet, pay you *forward* in the supernatural world according to the law of heaven.

Honor is heaven's highest, most-valued point of contract and trade. Without honor, there will be sin, flesh, and malice. But when honor is present, it's like doing business with Jesus: our interactions are filled with integrity, light, joy, truth, and generosity.

Our Savior was never terribly concerned with cash when he walked the earth, aside from warning us of its allure (Matthew 6:24; 1 Timothy 6:10). Contrary to popular belief, Jesus wasn't poor.[15] Yes, he gave up the privileges of the Godhead to take on flesh. But he had everything he needed in life—more than enough, in fact—because he relied on his Father for everything. He wore fine enough garments that Roman soldiers cast lots for them after his death (Matthew 27:35). He went to parties and dined with wealthy friends (Luke 5:29–32; 7:36–39; 11:37; 14:1–2). He pulled tax money from the mouths of *fish*, for heaven's sake (Matthew 17:27). Although he had access to kingdom resources on the earth (just as we do), Jesus knew honor was far more valuable than cash in the kingdom. This kept him at peace even in times of perceived lack (Matthew 8:20).

Although he had access to kingdom resources on the earth (just as we do), Jesus knew honor was far more valuable than cash in the kingdom.

You can be blessed with wealth and riches on the earth, but it doesn't mean you'll live in peace. When you live out of honor as currency, you'll know it's from heaven because there will be no strings attached in the natural world. You'll be willing to give unreasonably, willing to go without, willing to look like a fool for the sake of Jesus' gospel of honor. Because after all, everything you have is rightfully his—all honor, all glory, all blessing. Freely you have received—freely give (10:8).

The Ethics of Honor

Currency is more than bills, coins, and credit cards. Currency is a flow of life, a constant river of connection and virtue. From springs to streams, rivers to oceans, the current of currency flows from the Source himself—Jehovah Jireh, our provider. When you live a life of honor, you reap heavenly rewards now and in the afterlife. You gain favor, protection, blessings, and open doors.

According to Exodus 20:12, you will live well in the land—possessing a good life and preserved by the grace of God.

A life of honor requires a standard of ethics, because honor is an ethic in and of itself. It's an innate human value, a moral compass we all have whether we choose to acknowledge its true source or not. The ethics of honor involve integrity, truth, and faithfulness. Let's look at each of these more closely.

Integrity

Integrity is doing the right thing no matter what. As a noun, the word *integrity* refers to "the quality of being honest and having strong moral principles."[16] In short, integrity is moral uprightness. The fact that even secular cultures see value in operating with integrity only further proves the existence of our divine DNA. We were made to image God. And as his image-bearers, we inherently value doing the right thing. Until we don't.

When integrity is compromised (even in ways that don't seem to matter much in the moment), honor is squelched, and treachery reigns supreme. Compromise begets compromise in a relentless downward spiral, until one day we catch a glimpse of ourselves in the mirror and don't recognize our own faces. Instead of imaging God, we bear the graven images of our idols. In fear, we isolate ourselves from those who wear God's glory too brightly, and we rest in the comforting compromise of the complacent. Standing divided, we lose territory for the kingdom because our foundations lack integrity. The unity of the body of Christ hinges on our ability and willingness to operate with integrity in all things.

Truth

Truth is one of the most poorly defined terms in the English language. Dictionary definitions include "the state of being the case" and "a judgment, proposition, or idea that is true or accepted as true."[17] These definitions leave us wanting more because modern philosophy posits such a staunch relativistic and fluid approach to truth. We reject the concept of *the truth* and embrace the idea of *your truth*. Even God's truth as revealed in his inspired and inerrant Word gets lost in translation through denominational muddling, gross human error, and interpretative bias. Truth is no longer rooted in fact but in how we humans choose to believe in or accept it. Instead of being an existential source of reality, truth has become whatever we make it.

I believe reclaiming honor means reclaiming the Word of God as our primary source of truth. Our flesh may fail in vain attempts to excavate scriptural secrets in order to be right, but God is faithful to reveal treasures of heaven when we look to him and his Word as our only truth. Embracing God's truth requires humility, a letting go of everything you'd like to be true so you can embrace God's truth. Embracing the gospel truth requires faith that God's reality is far superior to the reality you're tempted to create on your own.

Faithfulness

Loyal. Reliable. Steadfast. A faithful spouse or friend. The faithful who can be counted on to pray and petition. As both a noun and an adjective, *faithful* describes an ethic marker that resembles the heart and character of God. He is faithful—and as he is, so are we. "Love has been perfected among us in this: that we may have boldness in the day of judgment; because as He is, so are we in this world" (1 John 4:17).

One of the most powerful paradoxes of human existence is this: *We are like God. But we are not God.* As faithfully as we may try to emulate Christ in our lives, we simply cannot walk it out perfectly. Though we are now perfect, holy, and blameless in God's sight, we have that standing only because of what Jesus did for us on the cross. His faithfulness all the way to the cross—obedience unto death—transcends human logic.

"But God demonstrates His own love toward us, in that while we were still sinners, Christ died for us" (Romans 5:8). While we were *still sinners*. Like Hosea with his wife, Gomer, the Lord has been faithful to us, showing such honor toward us even in our past, present, and future unfaithfulness (Hosea 3:1–5; 4:14). He saw beyond our wayward ways—and he became the Way for each and every one who believes in him so that each of us can achieve our fullest kingdom potential.

You have been saved by faith (Ephesians 2:8–9). Set free from sin and shame. Set free to rule and reign. The Lord's faithful know this, and they know that honor is the only way forward when stepping into God's best for their lives.

Jesus or Mammon?

If you're leaning into honor by reading this book, chances are you wouldn't hesitate to return a dropped $20 bill to a stranger. Somewhere deep down, we want to do the right thing simply because it's the right thing to do. At some level, you already know there is no lack in the kingdom, only abundance—which means others don't have to lose in order for you to gain. It seems basic, right? You might be shocked to learn how gray and murky the waters get when it comes to integrity with money in ministry.

While I was ministering at one megachurch, the pastor went out of his way to make it clear that he was doing me a favor by inviting me to speak. The backhanded compliments, the assumptive, abusive flattery…let's just say it wasn't subtle. The condescension compounded when, before I took the stage, he pulled me aside and callously slipped a $100 bill into my hand, as if he was concerned the love offering might not amount to enough. Yes, he could have just put the money in the offering plate like everyone else, but he seemed bent on making sure I knew where that particular $100 came from. My stomach turned. This flippant "I gotchu, bro" move felt wildly dishonoring, and my righteous anger began rising. Thanks to the Holy Spirit, I resisted the urge to throw the bill back in his face, which, although warranted, would certainly have been less than honorable. I refused to let dishonor breed dishonor in me.

Maintaining integrity with money in ministry must be both Spirit-led and board-approved. These aren't just legalistic boxes to check; they're helpful criteria to determine whether you're worshiping Jesus or mammon. The Holy Spirit will lead you into making honorable financial transactions alongside a council of anointed community members who help with discernment. Whether your transactions measure in the hundreds or in the hundreds of thousands, you'll have a crowd of witnesses to help you ensure that God's resources are truly being bestowed in honor.

Even surrounded by a healthy, discerning community, however, you will face situations where you have to make the call on your own. When this happens, lean into the words of Jesus in Matthew 5:3–12, where he describes the true nature of this upside-down kingdom we reside in as citizens of heaven:

> "Blessed are the poor in spirit, for theirs is the kingdom of heaven.
>
> Blessed are those who mourn, for they shall be comforted.

> Blessed are the meek, for they shall inherit the earth.
>
> Blessed are those who hunger and thirst for righteousness, for they shall be filled.
>
> Blessed are the merciful, for they shall obtain mercy.
>
> Blessed are the pure in heart, for they shall see God.
>
> Blessed are the peacemakers, for they shall be called sons of God.
>
> Blessed are those who are persecuted for righteousness' sake, for theirs is the kingdom of heaven.
>
> Blessed are you when they revile and persecute you, and say all kinds of evil against you falsely for My sake. Rejoice and be exceedingly glad, for great is your reward in heaven, for so they persecuted the prophets who were before you."

Humility. Compassion. Gentleness. Righteousness. Mercy. Purity. Peace. These "honor futures" are worthy of your investment. Yes, they provide perpetual, perennial, exponential, and compounding returns, but moreover, they are the way of Christ and worthy of emulation. Even if there were no earthly benefit to you (and trust me, there is!), having the mind of Christ and the purpose that comes with it is its own invaluable reward. Following Jesus and making continual honor investments will earn you compound interest over time.

Following Jesus and making continual honor investments will earn you compound interest over time.

What's more, you may even experience the supernatural benefits of showing honor to others. Similar to a credit card paid in full, you can earn reward points in the supernatural world that earn you more benefits, favors, and privileges. Can this manifest in hotel suites, frequent flyer miles, and discounts? Sure. But what you'll benefit from most is the outright favor of the Lord to help you fulfill your purpose. Sometimes this favor manifests instantaneously; sometimes it takes years to compound and produce a ready harvest. Whether you're valued by man or only by God, know that your reward is certain and secure in Christ. And your obedience will cause a ripple effect that will exponentially bless the people you love and lead.

In my experience, when you're faithful in the small things, you'll be entrusted with more and more. Right after ministering to the megachurch, I pulled the crumpled $100 bill from my pocket. Ole Ben Franklin's unmistakably frank, side-gazing eyes stared back at me as if to say, *Well, what are you going to do with me now?* What the enemy meant as a weapon to stir up offense, God turned around and used for good. I was able to use the money to bless my volunteer translator who had helped hundreds of people in the congregation find healing that day. He was worthy of his hire, and it was an honor to be able to honor him in this way.

The lesson here is that money is an amoral object. It is neither good nor evil until it is given a purpose—and even then, the purpose establishes the morality of it. Yes, the love of money may be the root of all evil (1 Timothy 6:10), but it's the intention *behind* the money that can cause us to stumble when it comes to honor. God fully redeemed that tainted gift of the $100 bill and blessed me to be a blessing to my translator, healing my own broken heart in the process. Since then, my ministry has received gifts upward of

$100,000 with no strings attached. I have reaped the harvest of God's rewards many times over, sometimes many seasons later. His timing is always perfect. I'm living proof that there is no scarcity in the kingdom and that we have access to God's full arsenal of resources on earth as we do in heaven.

Benefactors of Honor

Embracing honor as the currency of heaven will inevitably lead you toward becoming a benefactor of supernatural honor in the kingdom. This role isn't always about tangible financial resources, although money could play a part. Being a benefactor means offering help to a person or a cause as God leads you, providing resources, support, connections, and even protection. Several years ago, I was called to provide such a covering to a single mother with more than one child. I leveraged my connections to find a host family, help her secure employment, and give her a seat of honor within my congregation, thus opening doors for her and giving her a hope and a future.

For some, this benefactor/beneficiary relationship was complex at best. Some believed it inappropriate for me, a single man, to be the primary benefactor of a single mother. Fierce rumors flew—so fierce, in fact, that even *she* began to question me at times. I began pleading with the Lord, *How do I cover her without allowing this situation to bring too much damage?*

Jesus was faithful to remind me of all the women he had walked alongside in his earthly ministry—relationships that, in his day, would have been infinitely more controversial and inappropriate by cultural norms. Defending an adulterous woman? Speaking to a Samaritan woman at a public well? Letting a woman touch—let alone wash, kiss, and anoint—his feet?! *Scandalous!* (See Luke 7:36–50; John 4:1–42; 8:1–12.)

At the end of it all, I feared God more than I feared man. I knew he had called me to love this single mom with a deep, brotherly affection and to protect her as if she were my own flesh and blood. He had called me to dive deep into the controversial waters of grace, as Jesus did. I chose to honor her (and her extended family, whom I knew) by staying the course as her steward—opening doors for her and fighting for the relationship even when it became difficult. *Especially then.* This unwavering commitment and obedience eventually won over my community, sowing deep seeds of honor for more benefactors to rise up and bestow honor to their beneficiaries in the gentle way of Jesus.

The Currency of Babylon

Fearing God more than you fear man is a downright scary ideal. Obedience is almost always hard-won, and honor will always cost you something initially. If it doesn't? It's not really honor.

Just ask Daniel, a noble Jewish boy from Jerusalem enslaved by King Nebuchadnezzar II of Babylon. In and through his willing service to the king and eventually to Nebuchadnezzar's heirs (first King Belshazzar and then King Darius), Daniel was offered rich food, drink, and other cultural excesses that came strongly against his religious beliefs (Daniel 1:3–5). But unlike Esau, Daniel wasn't about to trade his inheritance for a bowl of soup (Genesis 25:29–34). He chose to honor the Lord, remaining undefiled and separating himself from the delicacies of compromise (Daniel 1:8).

Was eating veggies and water a tidbit awkward alongside connoisseurs of rich, fatty meat and sweet wine? You bet it was. In fact, Daniel's choice to maintain his religious convictions and resist the currency of Babylon could have been misconstrued as an act of dishonor. But when Daniel and his friends proved healthier and wiser for refusing the king's food, they were honored in Babylon by kings and men alike (vv. 8–20).

Daniel grew to love and honor King Darius, but he still refused to defile himself. And when Darius' jealous administrators gave him an ultimatum—worship only King Darius or die—Daniel refused to worship any earthly authority over the one true God. He was forced into a one-night stand with a den of hungry lions because of it (Daniel 6). By God's grace, Daniel remained unscathed, and Darius elevated him to a position of high honor in Babylon because he stood by his convictions. What's more, King Darius issued a decree that every part of his kingdom must fear and revere "the God of Daniel" (v. 26).

In the last days, some will call evil good and good evil (Isaiah 5:20). Babylon's currency is still being exchanged in every corner of creation, breeding confusion, malice, and straight-up sin. On the far side of the cross, this has much less to do with keeping kosher and much more to do with resisting the false honor of this world. Murder, adultery, theft, lies, and outright blasphemies are cloaked in disguises of justifiable honor, causing even the most faithful believers among us to question what God really says on the matter. Friend, this is the currency of Babylon: Robbing the rich to feed the poor. Stealing bread for your starving family. Commoditizing church to keep the doors open. Watching porn to maintain your virginity. Watering down the gospel to make it more palatable. The list goes on and on.

Yet this Babylonian currency is forever trumped by honor, the currency of heaven. Showing the ethics of honor—integrity, truth, and faithfulness—outweighs anything monetary or fiscal in the natural world. We get filled to overflowing. We lift others and God lifts us. Christ's success is our *collective* success.

Honor begets more and more honor—far more honor than money could ever buy. You gain the "more" of God through honor. What we do for others, God will do for us. He sees in secret and rewards in public. All heavenly business is powerfully transacted for God's kingdom in his currency of honor. When we invest in and steward honor faithfully, heaven's vault opens wide and exceptional favor is released.

Stewarding Honor

Investing in honor is one thing. Stewarding and sustaining it as part of a culture of honor is another. As you lean into the flow of heaven's currency—standing in truth, saying no to Babylon's delicacies, and doing the right thing no matter what—honor will begin to feel more natural to you. People will misunderstand you, but in time you'll realize it's not about them. It's not even about you. It's about the Lord—his ways, his truth, his glory. When you fear God more than you fear man, you'll look to him in all things instead of the world. And as you gaze upon God's majesty, his beauty will reflect in and through you as his image-bearer. You'll want to invest in heaven's currency not because you have to, but because you want to reap divine dividends. The currency of Babylon is worthless by comparison, and you're investing for a big return—eternal life in Christ!

These kinds of returns will require you to live like no one else does so you can live with your Creator—forever and ever, amen. It means staying classy when others go ashy. It means being a gentleman or a lady when others are being Neanderthals. It means being a strong, solid leader even as the world around you crumbles on a weak and faulty foundation.

Honorable Reflections

What was the hardest thing you've ever had to do, but you did it and God blessed you?

Will you truly gain the world if you have to sell your soul?

What practical benefits and rewards come from investing in and stewarding honor?

How does honor weigh in against the earthly currencies of Babylon?

Are you operating in the currency of heaven or the currency of this earth?

5

A Spirit of Honor

For a bishop must be blameless, as a steward of God, not self-willed, not quick-tempered, not given to wine, not violent, not greedy for money, but hospitable, a lover of what is good, sober-minded, just, holy, self-controlled, holding fast the faithful word as he has been taught, that he may be able, by sound doctrine, both to exhort and convict those who contradict.

TITUS 1:7–9 NKJV

Hospitality is not to change people, but to offer them space where change can take place.

HENRI NOUWEN

I was eleven years old when my birth mother left.

Before you rush to my defense in righteous offense, you should know how very much I honor my mother and the decisions she felt she was forced into. She is one of the most artistic, vibrant, charismatic, electric women you'll ever meet. The last of her siblings, my mom was intensely favored in her family of origin. Her affluent, much older parents nicknamed their little miracle *Min*, which translates as "clever" but also implies stunning beauty. Before Mom married my father, she was an award-winning artist in Korea. She was the life of the party, a truly free spirit. Dad's strict educational background and upbringing, as well as his "lowbrow" *Lim* surname, made him an unlikely choice for courtship. In Korean culture, certain last names and families of regional origin are looked down upon due to lower social status. My father's last name and region of origin weren't favorable as a whole—not because of his personal actions but simply because of their social status. Yet my father and mother married anyway, moved to the States, and launched a family and a ministry at the same time.

Things were tense in our young family. All of a sudden, ministry didn't suit my mom well, nor did being the wife of a Korean American pastor. She felt like a slave—a shadow of her former self. I was a momma's boy, and I often provided comfort and care in the aftermath of my parents' many disputes. The verbal abuse began to escalate, and Mom would occasionally pack her bags in dramatic fashion and leave for a day or two to teach my father a lesson. She always came back. Until one day she didn't.

The anguish of abandonment was raw and real for my older brother, Howard, and me. I'm sure it was for my father too. But in our family's false culture of honor, we were never given permission to acknowledge the pain—let alone heal from it or the divorce that followed. To speak of it at all would have brought great dishonor on our family. The rising tension made me feel unwelcome and unsafe in my own home: the atmosphere festered with loneliness and isolation. Perhaps you've felt the same in a season of abandonment. The smoldering ashes of my former existence still hung as a thick cloud in the air, but life pressed on unapologetically, as it often does.

Just a year later, to the surprise and delight of the church elders, my father remarried. This marriage to a woman named Crystal was "a match made in heaven" devised by mutual pastor friends. Dad was eager to remarry quickly to preserve his role in ministry and his good family name. It was Crystal's first marriage, and she bravely stepped into a broken home with two preteen boys. This kind of arrangement was almost unheard of in Korean culture, but she stepped in with humility and grace.

Dad and Crystal got busy getting to know one another, and my brother and I adjusted to the abrupt newness of it all. Howard rebelled initially, reluctant to accept Crystal and regularly reminding her, "You're not my mom!"

I missed my mom too, but I resisted the urge to mimic my big brother, because I saw something so very different in Crystal's spirit. She was meek, generous, and compassionate. She was patient and kind, but she was also firm and steadfast. She made me feel safe and free by giving me clear, healthy, and consistent boundaries. She would never replace *my* mother—but she stepped in to be *a* mother to my lonely and wounded spirit.

To say I did everything I could in those early years to please Crystal is an understatement. My broken, orphaned spirit operated in perpetual desperation because I was terrified that she would leave like my mother had. Dad seemed different, but who knew for sure? My brother was in all-out rebellion, although he did come around eventually. Cheryl was the only safe person in my life, and I clung to her desperately. Everything she asked, I did. Everything she said, I wholeheartedly agreed with. I even started eating the vilest of vegetables—tomatoes, salad, and even *kimchi*—in hopes that she would choose to stay. She delighted in me and I in her.

Deep down, however, I kept my broken heart braced for impact. Why would Crystal want to stay with me when nobody else did? Why should she have to put up with my family and me when she could do so much better? I would lie awake at night and wonder, *What in the world am I going to do when she's gone?* As our broken family desperately began rebuilding our relationships, I still felt miserably alone. We'll come back to that story in just a minute, after a look at how honoring people can mean receiving them into your heart and life as Crystal did with me.

A Facet of the Holy Spirit

A spirit of honor is one of the many powerful facets of the Holy Spirit's character. It is vital to give and receive honor, because it makes both the giver and the recipient better people for it. It calls forth the underdogs and empowers champions into their kingdom destiny. Embodying this spirit means not only honoring the grace on other people's lives but also being aware of and attentive to their needs. In a word? It means *hospitality.*

> ***It is vital to give and receive honor, because it makes both the giver and the recipient better people for it.***

Hospitality is very prevalent in Korean, Arabic, Jewish, and Middle Eastern cultures, where it becomes your duty to host visitors and refugees from other lands. The Old Testament mandate for showing honor to strangers, foreigners, and newcomers is made abundantly clear in Leviticus 19:34: "'The stranger who dwells among you shall be to you as one born among you, and you shall love him as yourself; for you were strangers in the land of Egypt: I am the Lord your God.'" This verse starts out with an occasionally inconvenient truth and continues with two powerfully potent reasons why showing honor in hospitality is critical.

An inconvenient truth:

> "The stranger who dwells among you shall be to you as one born among you, and you shall love him as yourself."

Reason 1: You know what it's like.

> "For you were strangers in the land of Egypt."

Imagine a time when you were lost, a stranger in a foreign land. New schools. New churches. New cities and communities and callings. No matter who you are or where you're from or what you've experienced, you have no doubt personally benefited from a spirit of honor in the form of hospitality. God willing, you could find yourself in that same place again as God calls you deeper into the great unknown. As we have received the Spirit's grace freely, we must be willing to give it all the more—outdoing one another in honor.

Reason 2: You know God says so.

> "I am the Lord your God."

In case this wasn't already abundantly clear, let me make it plain: God is God—and you are not. And ultimately, he gets the last word when it comes to honor. You might be able to reason away honor in every earthly instance, but sometimes God has us show honor for no earthly reason at all—other than that he has commanded us to do so in his name. "Thus saith the Lord." Period. As if that weren't already enough.

Honoring people by receiving them into your heart, your home, and your life is risky. Yet it's a risk we must be willing to take as image-bearers of God, even in times when people seek to exploit the very hospitality we are called to show. Hosting people well is a by-product of hosting the Holy Spirit. Whether you're entertaining angels or not, hosting a man or woman of God may also mean hosting a move of God. Are you willing? One Shunammite woman was:

> Now it happened one day that Elisha went to Shunem, where there was a notable woman, and she persuaded him to eat some food. So it was, as often as he passed by, he would turn in there to eat some food. And she said to her husband, "Look now, I know that this is a holy man of God, who passes by us regularly. Please, let us make a small upper room on the wall; and let us put a bed for him there, and a table and a chair and a lampstand; so it will be, whenever he comes to us, he can turn in there."
>
> And it happened one day that he came there, and he turned in to the upper room and lay down there. Then he said to Gehazi his servant, "Call this Shunammite woman." When he had called her, she stood before him. And he said to him, "Say now to her, 'Look, you have been concerned for us with all this care. What can I do for you? Do you want me to speak on your behalf to the king or to the commander of the army?'"

> She answered, "I dwell among my own people."
>
> So he said, "What then is to be done for her?"
>
> And Gehazi answered, "Actually, she has no son, and her husband is old."
>
> So he said, "Call her." When he had called her, she stood in the doorway. Then he said, "About this time next year you shall embrace a son."
>
> And she said, "No, my lord. Man of God, do not lie to your maidservant!"
>
> But the woman conceived, and bore a son when the appointed time had come, of which Elisha had told her. (2 Kings 4:8–17)

God worked through the prophet Elisha not only to give the Shunammite woman the gift of a son; he also raised that same son from the dead through his prophet just a few short years later (vv. 18–37). Never underestimate the power of hospitality. It redeems and restores dignity, value, and even life itself.

To continue my earlier story, I'm thrilled to share that I was wrong about Crystal. She never left me as my birth mother did, although nobody would have blamed her if she had. It wasn't long after she turned me on to veggies that even within the comfort of her love and hospitality, I backslid, falling into a life of drugs, crime, and seemingly endless trouble. A fiery woman of God and a fierce prayer warrior, Crystal fought for me as her own son—even when it got hard. *Especially then.* She endured my rebellious manipulations, turned the other cheek countless times, and still continued honoring me—pursuing and believing the best about me at all costs. She mined the gold from my wayward spirit and won me over time and again with a spirit of unshakable hospitality.

Crystal was a safe-haven home to me in and through my darkest years, and I know she is part of the reason I am alive, breathing, and declaring the gospel today. Fast-forward a decade or two, and she does so much more than just cheer me on. She works alongside me and travels with me as my righteous and capable right hand in my ministry, bringing a bit of home with us wherever we go.

Like the Shunammite woman, Crystal received me as a son.

Like the Shunammite woman, she watched me fall into certain death.

And like the Shunammite woman, she witnessed me being resurrected into fullness of life.

Her hospitality kept on giving.

The honor Crystal showed me from when I was a young age redeemed the abandonment, divorce, abuse, narcissism, violence, and hopelessness the enemy tried to use to destroy me. Crystal's willingness to show honor redeemed it all. Fear can be a powerful motivator, but love triumphs over fear every time. In the midst of a broken family and a broken life, honor came.

A Lifestyle of Hospitality

A spirit of honor is both a facet and a virtue of the Holy Spirit. It's living a lifestyle of hospitality, generosity, and thanksgiving that empowers and brings life. A spirit of honor doesn't come naturally to us, and for good reason. Honor isn't natural. It's supernatural. Like grace, honor is something that must be revealed by the Lord, received in faith, and released over others in a truly divine pay-it-forward sequence.

Honor can be learned, but it's more easily *caught*—it's quite contagious! Spend any amount of time with others who are walking in a spirit of honor, and some of that spirit is bound to rub off on you. And once you taste and see how good honor is, you'll want more of it so you can spend your life giving it away. Honor divinely aligns you to your higher calling, which is first to honor the Lord and then to honor others.

A spirit of honor appeals to the hungry because honor is attractive. When you carry the grace of honor, you shine brightly in the room. People gravitate to you, and they don't know why. It's not charisma or personality; it's not man-made or fleshly. It's true honor, a virtue that has been birthed through Holy-Spirit fire. When you see it, you'll want your heart to be set ablaze with it too.

When King David's heir, Solomon, rose to rule, he asked God for one thing: wisdom (1 Kings 3:5–9). God gave it to him liberally, and he grew in prosperity and fame across the land. The queen of Sheba, a wise and wealthy ruler herself, heard all about it and had to see it for herself. More than that, she wanted to put Solomon to the test with tough questions. Most kings would probably drown in sweat trying to answer them. But in 1 Kings 10, we see that the wisdom of this Israelite king simply blew the Queen of Sheba's mind away. The honor, gifts, and unmatched hospitality he bestowed upon her far surpassed her humble-by-comparison housewarming gifts of gold, spices, jewels, and sandalwood that she brought his way: "Now King Solomon gave the queen of Sheba all she desired, whatever she asked, besides what Solomon had given her according to the royal generosity" (v. 13). The queen discovered firsthand that Solomon was everything people said he was and more—and that his God was worthy to be praised. She honored Solomon, he honored her, and the Lord honored them both.

After Sheba's openhearted queen visited Solomon, she left a different person. She overcame her initial skepticism and left eager to tell the whole world about him. The king's kindness, generosity, and wisdom won her over completely, and she affirmed Solomon's anointing and good name across the land. His kind of hospitality should be our gold standard when hosting and receiving strangers, foreigners, and newcomers into our home or community. They need to leave even better than they came because of the honor they receive from us as we live out a lifestyle of hospitality.

Hosting and Receiving

There once was a traveling evangelist to whom I casually mentioned in passing, "Hey, if you're ever in L.A., look me up!"

You'd better believe he did. He asked to come stay with me for a week. With a spirit of honor, I gave him my enthusiastic and expectant *Yes!*

I'm sure this evangelist took me at my word and expected a warm meal and a place simply to rest his head for a bit. But I knew that the bare minimum simply wouldn't do for such a man of God as this. He spent his days—every breath of his life—pouring into others for the sake of the gospel, making Christ known in communities around the world. And I knew this was an opportunity for my community and me to honor him in the eyes of God and man. I was blessed to be able to lavish love on this precious man—covering extravagant meals, evenings on the town, a brand-new wardrobe, and even his outstanding bills and ministry expenses while he was in my care. I fully admit, I cannot always give so extravagantly. But in this season, because of my willingness, God gave me access to all the riches of Solomon to give away freely in Jesus' name.

This evangelist deserved the very best I could offer him—not just because of who he was or what he had done for the kingdom but because of who we both were in Christ. And so, I wanted him to feel like a guest of the Lord in my house. Honoring others by hosting them is arguably the most perfect representation of the *shalom* of God here in the natural world. Our very hearts are the abode of heaven, where we are not only image-bearers (a reflection) but also image-carriers (a habitation). The Holy Spirit has set up residence inside you. And you, as a temple of the living God, are meant to provide sanctuary, solace, and Sabbath rest to those who come knocking at your door.

This beautiful opportunity to extend honor through hosting this evangelist was perhaps so precious to me because of how often I am on the receiving end of honor when it comes to ministry. I'm on the road forty-five to forty-seven weeks out of the year, bringing the Lord's good news, great joy, and full healing in Jesus' name to faith communities around the world. My first commitment as a senior pastor is to my local church flock, so I've made a commitment to be there for Sunday services as much as possible. From wherever I am, I catch the first flight available on Sunday morning to make it to our afternoon service. Our elders and leaders agree that our mandate as a ministry is from Southern California to the world. Itinerant pastoring may seem glamorous to some, but some of us are rarely home or don't even *have* a home. In fact, many of us need a place to rest our own heads, at least for a season. Jesus needed this and admittedly struggled to find it (Matthew 8:20). Why wouldn't we? Needing hospitality, however, doesn't excuse us from walking in a spirit of honor, even when we have nothing left to give. Whether you're receiving people into your home or receiving the kindness and compassion of a home willing to host *you*, honor is key.

As a guest, your responsibility is to leave your hosts better off than when you came. You may not have the riches of the queen of Sheba to bring as housewarming gifts, but the spiritual gifts you bestow on your hosts make a measurable difference. Trust your hosts to provide for your needs, but step in quickly to help with meals, pay for groceries, watch children, and minister to those in need. Clean up after yourself and others. Don't complain about the food or lodging. Buy flowers or leave handwritten notes. Offer a listening ear and a helping hand. Pitch in with household chores and projects. To be a blessing to your hosts, share with them whatever wisdom, insight, and blessings you carry.

And above all, *read the room*. Stay keenly aware of the circumstances surrounding you and open your heart to be a conduit of grace. Resist the urge to correct or be right. Honor the traditions of the house. Lay down your life like a servant, acting as if you were in the palace of a great king or queen. It sounds so basic, but these simple acts break off a spirit of entitlement in our hearts or in the perceptions of the ones who risk it all to open their homes, lives, and hearts to us. Leave your hosts truly sorry to see you go, and you will be welcome back anytime into the blessing of kingdom community.

Honor is the *shalom* of God. The abode of heaven. The habitation of the Lord. Do you embody these things? Host or guest, there is one critical question to ask yourself when it comes to hospitality manifested in a spirit of honor: *Would God want to visit with me?*

Because of our abundance of information via social media, our connection with various different cultures, and our ability to sympathize with others, I believe our generation is uniquely equipped to create places of safety, love, hospitality, and honor. We are uniquely equipped to create homes, families, and communities of hospitality that embody the Holy Spirit's presence—environments committed to restoring and refreshing guests and hosts alike. But if we're honest, even when they have the best of intentions, sometimes Christians don't do hospitality very well. We host with the expectation that our guests will be not only civil but grateful, thankful, and blessed beyond measure. We stay with the expectation that our hosts will be not only welcoming and selfless but will anticipate our every need (and then some). All too often, we focus on the flesh, the self—and we miss prime opportunities to act as Christ's hands and feet to our guests and our hosts alike.

There's a reason why the Holy Scriptures recount Jesus encouraging us to pack light:

> "Take nothing for the journey, neither staffs nor bag nor bread nor money; and do not have two tunics apiece.
>
> Whatever house you enter, stay there, and from there depart. And whoever will not receive you, when you go out of that city, shake off the very dust from your feet as a testimony against them." (Luke 9:3–5)

We aren't meant to plan for contingencies or eventualities. We aren't meant to put up walls and draw lines in the sand. We are meant to establish trust long before it's ever earned—to trust God to do what *he* wants to when *he* wants to. We're meant to be his willing vessels no matter the outcome.

What if our hosts could be blown away at how keeping us in their home lightened their load and enriched their lives?

What if our guests could have life-changing experiences and identity-driven breakthrough while in our care?

What if the sole purpose of being blessed and honored is to, in turn, honor and bless?

We could not only prove our elders wrong when it comes to honor being lost in our generation; we could also show them who we really are: one with God in Christ by the power of the Holy Spirit, Christ made manifest within a collective spirit of honor that we're all meant to carry as image-bearers.

What if the sole purpose of being blessed and honored is to, in turn, honor and bless?

When it comes to honor, be willing to give *and* willing to receive. Let your peace rest on others regardless of whether you receive them or they receive you. Trust that your heavenly Father will sustain you. Honor your hospitality counterparts by outdoing them in honor. Go out of your way to bless them. Kindness leads people to repentance—and so does honor. So much so that some people may actually fear you when you walk in it, because honor can be terrifying to people who don't walk in it. Your accusers won't dare speak against you because honor terrifies the enemy. Hospitality is your opportunity to be one who makes Satan shake in his shoes. He will see the profound ways in which you honor others, and he will tremble.

Nicodemuses

Sometimes a word from the Lord isn't meant for public consumption. This can be difficult for growing prophetic leaders to understand because it takes wisdom and discernment. When God speaks, he doesn't always mean it for the masses. Sometimes he speaks straight to our heart (even concerning another individual), and we're meant to ponder these things in our heart as Mary did

(Luke 2:19). Instead of proclaiming it to the masses as a corporate word, we can treasure a word until the Lord asks us to release it in a broader way.

That said, when it comes to honor, our public and private behaviors need to align purposefully, intentionally, and strategically. And when we're presented with an opportunity to show honor by revealing a word from God concerning a person, we need to be quick to obedience, even when it puts our own reputation at risk.

Just ask Nicodemus, a prominent Jewish rabbi, Pharisee, and esteemed member of the Sanhedrin. His unyielding curiosity prompted him to meet face-to-face with Jesus in secret, away from the prying eyes and judging hearts of his fellow religious leaders (John 3:1–21).

You might identify with Nicodemus' initial skepticism of Jesus. Any man claiming to be the Messiah in that day was typically seen either as a false prophet or a delusional madman. You may also sympathize with the enormous risk to Nicodemus in speaking with Jesus. If his contemporaries found out, he would lose his position, his family, his reputation, his faith, and possibly his life for being affiliated with such a radical man. Even *considering* entertaining Jesus would be considered blasphemy. So he met with his soon-to-be Savior under the cover of night—in a meeting that would change him forever. He marveled at Christ's baffling invitation to be "born again." Nicodemus called Jesus "Rabbi," a term of great respect, and acknowledged him as a prophet, bestowing profound honor on Jesus as this Jewish religious leader drank deeply from the well of Jesus' teachings (v. 2).

At least in private.

Publicly, Nicodemus wasn't yet willing to risk his neck for Jesus. Even though his heart transformation had already begun,

Nicodemus did not boldly proclaim Jesus as the Messiah before men. It's worth noting that he once subtly defended Jesus when the Sanhedrin tried to arrest him without cause (7:50–51). But when the Sanhedrin immediately accused Nicodemus of sympathizing with Jesus, the exchange ended abruptly.

Intellectually, Nicodemus knew who Jesus really was, and he even believed in Christ spiritually. But it took time for his heart and mind to muster the courage to sacrifice everything and follow him publicly.

I admit that I can relate to Nicodemus' plight. But as a millennial pastor and prophetic voice, I can also identify with Jesus in this highly relevant biblical account. I've had several Nicodemuses in my life and ministry—people who affirm, celebrate, and champion me privately but who see me as too dangerous to publicly honor and align with. They may build me up and flatter me in secret, but they refuse to acknowledge my ministry. And they even speak poorly of me in public.

This is not the Lord's way of honor. He sees what we do in secret and honors us in public (Matthew 6:17–18). He affirms us in the secret place and then champions us before men—unashamed of who we are because he has made us holy and blameless by his own sacrifice. Can you imagine if the Lord lavished love on you in private but shamed or ignored you in public? Certainly not! Jesus was willing to go to hell and back again to claim you as his own, and he would do it again.

Fear is what keeps honor in the shadows. But love, God's perfect love, casts out fear (1 John 4:18). And in the absence of fear, we rise up with boldness for the gospel. Nicodemus came to Jesus as he was, with doubts and questions and fears. He may have been slow to proclaim what he believed about our Lord, but eventually he came around. He not only defended Jesus publicly; he testified at Jesus' trial before Pilate.[18] Most notably, Nicodemus was present to grieve with friends, family, disciples, and other believers the day Jesus died. He joined forces with Joseph of Arimathea, another former "secret believer," to request Jesus' body and bury it (John 19:38–42). It's worth noting that the tomb they laid him in was fit for royalty. Matthew's gospel suggests it was Joseph's *own* tomb (Matthew 27:59–60). The two men risked everything to honor their Lord at his death, breaking away from Jewish leadership, knowing Jesus was the only way, the only truth, and the only life (John 14:6).

Choosing to honor people will cost you something. But a spirit of honor—a facet of the Holy Spirit—will guide you in bestowing honor in this earthly realm. It won't always make sense. It's risky and occasionally dangerous. It requires a level of reckless love that we could never muster in our own strength. Honor is a supernatural flow of grace. And those who honor God by honoring people will receive the Spirit's fire, favor, peace, and power in ways that will transform them forever.

What are you waiting for? Embrace hospitality as a kingdom virtue. Entertain an angel or two or twenty! Receive honor and blessing so you can honor and bless. Step into the honor, flow with boldness, and see where the Spirit takes you.

Honorable Reflections

How is hospitality connected to carrying a spirit of honor?

Have you ever honored someone privately but not publicly? How did you—or how will you—correct this, as Nicodemus did by honoring Jesus in the end?

When people honor you with their hospitality, what do you do to lighten the load and enrich the lives of your hosts?

Consider your role as a host or guest. Are you showing honor in whatever community God places you in?

6

Vessels of Honor

But in a great house there are not only vessels of gold and silver, but also of wood and clay, some for honor and some for dishonor. Therefore if anyone cleanses himself from the latter he will be a vessel for honor, sanctified and useful for the Master, prepared for every good work.

2 Timothy 2:20–21 NKJV

God is not looking for gold vessels or silver vessels. He is looking for willing vessels.

Kathryn Kuhlman

As image-bearers, we are (by definition) created to carry something. We are not only meant to reflect our Maker by bearing his image; we are also meant to be carriers of his presence, carriers of the Lord Himself. Perhaps this is why the Scriptures refer to followers of Christ as *vessels*—"jars of clay" (2 Corinthians 4:7) meant to carry the power and authority of God until our bodies return to the dust and our souls are fully glorified in his presence.

Now, God is God and we are not—which means we are *carriers* of his glory, not originators or producers of it. It is God who heals, restores, and makes all things new. It is God who bestows honor so that we might not only pay it forward but also give it right back to him, the only one who is truly worthy of receiving it.

In Paul's second letter to his protégé, Timothy, Paul explains this phenomenon in the verses from 2 Timothy 2 you just read at the start of this chapter. Paul calls us vessels for honor if we are sanctified, useful, and prepared for every good work. So let me ask you these questions:

- What is your current condition as a vessel of honor?
- Is your silver polished?
- Are your clay seams cracking?
- Are your wooden handles starting to dry-rot?
- Are you perhaps feeling lost, dirty, or forgotten?
- Furthermore, what "latter" thing might you need to be cleansed of?

In answer to that last question, profane and idle babblings, false prophecy, and iniquity, certainly (vv. 14–19). If you read to the end of Paul's chapter, he makes it perfectly clear what needs to go from your life so you can be the vessel of honor you were created to be:

> *Flee also youthful lusts*; but pursue righteousness, faith, love, peace with those who call on the Lord out of a pure heart. *But avoid foolish and ignorant disputes*, knowing that they generate strife. And a servant of the Lord *must not quarrel but be gentle to all, able to teach, patient, in humility* correcting those who are in opposition, if God perhaps will grant

> them repentance, so that they may know the truth, and that they may come to their senses and escape the snare of the devil, having been taken captive by him to do his will. (vv. 22–26, emphasis added)

As a vessel, you must be equipped to carry the honor God wants to give you and others. Paul's words offer keen insight into this equipping process, teaching us what it will really take to become a vessel of honor. It will require one of the purest (and most difficult) displays of honor imaginable: honoring yourself.

Honor the Soul

Because Jesus defeated sin and cleansed us from all unrighteousness, we are all worthy of honor. And it's not because of what we've done but because of what he did. This creates a complex version of reality in the natural world: someone can be worthy of honor but not always do honorable things.

Paul spoke to this reality through a beautifully tragic allegory in his letter to the church in Rome: "I do not understand what I do. For what I want to do I do not do, but what I hate I do" (Romans 7:15 NIV; cf. vv. 16–20). Paul wasn't speaking to his current personal reality so much as to the collective state of the church, which was clinging to sin as an entirely unavoidable eventuality.

Are you ready for the truth? It's a bit shocking, but it's key to unlocking your full potential as a vessel of honor in the kingdom of God: when Jesus died, your sinful nature died with him. Yes, really.

Through Jesus' death and resurrection, the curse of Eden was broken, and you were restored to your rightful identity as an image-bearer of the living God—pure, holy, and blameless in his sight. Not because of what *you* did but because of what *Jesus* did for you.

Is it fair? No. Does it make sense? No. Is it hands-down the *best* news humankind has ever received? Yes, yes, *yes* and amen!

As a perfectly polished, sealed, useful, and beautifully adorned vessel, you carry the very Spirit of God within you—and you are capable of pouring out a spirit of honor wherever you go. As a vessel of honor, what you choose to carry matters because it becomes a transferable legacy, multiplied throughout the generations. What you watch, whom you listen to and the company you keep, how you celebrate and grieve, how you work and rest—it *all* matters.

When you carry honor, honor will overflowingly manifest and multiply. Same goes with grace, peace, joy, gratitude, and compassion. But when you carry dishonor, dishonor will overflowingly manifest and multiply. Same goes with lust, greed, wrath, despair, and pride. When you carry vices in your spirit, it doesn't just hurt you; it hurts the ones you're uniquely called to love, lead, and honor. I'm convinced this is why it seems that honor has been "lost" a little bit more in every emerging generation. While any generation can reclaim honor, I'm convinced that making the choice to carry honor is how my generation will reclaim it, in Jesus' name.

Becoming a vessel of honor is an inside job—one that starts with yourself. Honoring yourself certainly isn't selfish, because we must surrender to the reality that we can't give away what we don't have in our possession. God, in his infinite grace, bestowed honor upon us at creation. Yes, we may have lost it for a bit. But Jesus reclaimed it for us on the cross by becoming the propitiation for our sin, regaining the goodwill of our Father through his loving and shockingly honoring sacrifice (1 John 2:1–2). You are worthy of honor because Christ is worthy of honor, and to deny yourself that God-given honor is a recipe for legalism with a side of shame.

Honoring yourself looks a lot like self-care—or more appropriately, like *soul-care*. I'm not talking about luxurious spa excursions or extravagant "treat yourself" days (although they could play a part, God willing). I'm talking about taking intentional care of your mental, emotional, physical, environmental, spiritual, recreational, and social well-being by choosing to honor the gold God has placed deep within you as his beloved child, his image-bearer. Investing in soul-care means honoring your space, your time, your boundaries, your worth, and your oneness with the Lord. Soul-care is stewarding yourself as a vessel of honor, making sure you are poised and positioned to be God's honor conduit.

Soul-care is stewarding yourself as a vessel of honor, making sure you are poised and positioned to be God's honor conduit.

The sad reality is that many believers refuse to receive God's rich, heavy *kāḇôḏ* of honor because their personal vessels need stewarding. Instead, they take a self-deprecating, self-loathing approach and call it humility. They walk in what is sometimes referred to as "the overlap of the ages," an already/not yet mindset that still screams, *Christ is worthy, and I am not!* The problem with this widely held belief is that it limits our access to the spiritual blessings and kingdom resources that are already ours by biblical definition. We are saved (Ephesians 2:8). Adopted (Romans 8:15). Redeemed (Ephesians 1:7). Sanctified (1 Corinthians 1:2). And yes, even raised up with Christ (Ephesians 2:6). And yet, like Eve when she was tempted by the serpent, we, too, sometimes assume that God must be holding out on us—that we have something more to hope for beyond reconciled oneness with him.

Deep down, we don't believe that what Jesus did was enough. Therefore, we believe that we, too, are not enough.

This false narrative creates a paralyzing theological tension that keeps believers from receiving the upgrades and promotions necessary to advance the kingdom of God in this realm. When we don't honor ourselves enough to honor the call of God on our lives, we will stay stuck. Frustration will fester, resentment will grow, and we will cease to be vessels of honor. We will become barriers to honor instead—withholding, slandering, and condemning—and we will perpetuate a generational curse that is counter to our divine DNA. We were made in honor in order to carry honor; we were blessed to be a blessing. Anything less *dishonors* the One who formed us into vessels in the first place.

Being a vessel of honor isn't about being worthy. It's about being willing. So let me ask you these questions:

- Are you willing?
- Are you willing to care for your own soul so you might also care for others?
- Are you willing to flee from victim and orphan spirits that perpetuate self-loathing?
- Are you willing to allow yourself to be filled to overflowing?

Honor God. Honor yourself. Honor others. Freely and without hesitation. This is what it means to be a *willing* vessel.

Honor Offerings

Can you put a price on salvation? It once cost me $15,000.

One February, my ministry team helped facilitate and finance a conference out West. Now, there is always some financial risk in planning events and gatherings, and more than once, the Lord has asked me to take huge leaps of faith, trusting that his provision would come in his timing. It always has. And I believed it always would. So when conference weekend yielded a much lower attendance than we all expected, I refused to panic. I just knew the Lord would come through in one way or another. A wildly generous love offering. A few conference latecomers with deep pockets. Dollar bills raining from the sky, perhaps? Maybe. And why not? God loves to show off. I didn't concern myself with how God would provide. I just knew he would and stayed focused on the precious souls he had brought to us for salvation, deliverance, and blessing.

The conference was pure fire. We were a small and mighty crew for the Lord, and his presence was palpable. Bodies were healed. Chains were broken. Souls were set free. Leaders and attendees alike sensed the Lord's favor as his cloud of glory grew thick among our ranks. As the weekend wrapped up and our honored guests packed up and came for their checks, the reality finally hit me that we hadn't made budget. We hadn't missed it by a little bit, but by *thousands*.

Cognitive dissonance crouched at my door, begging me to entertain the thought that I had somehow misheard the Lord about this conference. The voice was *loud: You got greedy, Ben. You're not a faithful steward. You should know better.*

Instead of entertaining those icy lies, I leaned into the warm, affirming embrace of my heavenly Father. I tuned in to his voice, and he spoke truth to my mind, body, and soul: *You hear me so well, Ben. You can trust my provision.*

And then he said something I'll never forget: *Ben, you ARE my provision.*

After a quick phone call with my board, I pulled out my personal checkbook, wrote "Fifteen thousand and 00/100" on the line, and slipped it into the proverbial plate to cover the remainder of the conference spread. The provision I was believing so fervently for? I *was* that provision. It wasn't what I expected. I can honestly say it's not what I *wanted*—at least, I wouldn't have raised my hand for it at the outset. But there it was—a chance for me to pour out the honor I'd been given and in turn honor God with everything I had.

That gift became one of the greatest joys of my life and ministry. I was so blessed to be in a season where I had both the means and the motivation to honor the Lord's plans by stepping in to be the solution I wanted to see. It changed the way I prayed for provision going forward, because it was no longer a scarcity-riddled plea for "enough" to get by; rather, it was a request to be filled to overflowing. For some, a conference budget deficit would be mortifying, an admission of some kind of earthly failure, negligence, or naivety. But supernaturally, I was able to participate in the bringing of the kingdom—not just by teaching, preaching, and praying at the conference, but by giving personally, generously, selflessly, and with joy! I was able to honor our guests richly and strategically invest in what God was up to in the region. I gave God my emphatic *Yes!* by saying, *Here I am, God—use me.*

Being a vessel of honor is recognizing that *everyone* is made for the miraculous, the supernatural, and the extraordinary. But it's our job to build on the ordinary—to be faithful with the common, the everyday, the usual—to build the solid character and inner resolve it takes to demonstrate honor.

Being a vessel of honor is recognizing that everyone is made for the miraculous, the supernatural, and the extraordinary.

If you think my "dollar bills raining from the sky" musing was a little arrogant, consider the only miracle Jesus performed that was recorded in all four Gospels. When a little lad gave all he had—five loaves of bread and two fish, to be exact—it was more than enough to feed five thousand people who were hungry for the Word—and then some (Matthew 14:13–21; Mark 6:31–44; Luke 9:12–17; John 6:1–14). Emptying my savings to cover conference costs pales in comparison to this young boy's sacrifice for his Savior. But in both cases, Jesus took our all and multiplied it exponentially, honoring us and the recipients of his provision.

God could have covered that conference spread six ways from Sunday, but he chose me. He wanted to know if I would be faithful with an ordinary act of obedience in stewardship so he could launch me into extraordinary provision. Since that conference, God has repaid my financial gift many times over and has given me increased boldness in believing for—and being—his provision. That moment of humility has generated exponential supernatural glory in my life—an out-of-the-box, out-of-this-world existence. I dare say this extraordinary life is available to all of us, *if* we are fully surrendered to him.

If Jesus made it so *all* could be saved, God intends for us *all* to operate confidently in our identities as image-bearers, regardless of our vocation or role. Ministerially, you may be a conference keynote speaker or an usher. Both are needed and valuable. Vocationally, you may be a Fortune 500 CEO or a stay-at-home parent. Both are needed and valuable. But don't settle for less than God's will. God is sovereign and in control, but the form, fit, and function of your life's vocations are up to you to decide. Not your parents. Not the government. Not a system, power, or principality. Just you.

> Do not be deceived, God is not mocked; for whatever a man sows, that he will also reap. For he who sows to his flesh will of the flesh reap corruption, but he who sows to the Spirit will of the Spirit reap everlasting life. And let us not grow weary while doing good, for in due season we shall reap if we do not lose heart. (Galatians 6:7–9)

If you want to be a vessel of honor, you must die to entitlement. Nobody owes you anything. Instead, be mature in your identity, taking ownership of what is true and what is not. Walk forth as a valiant vessel of grace and honor, showing the world what life could be like when you honor God, honor others, and honor yourself.

Much Given, Much Required

I'd be doing you a great disservice if I didn't let you know that God expects more from those who seek to be honorable. Luke makes it abundantly clear in his gospel that when it comes to honor, the more you receive, the more you're meant to give away: "For everyone to whom much is given, from him much will be required; and to whom much has been committed, of him they will ask the more" (Luke 12:48 NKJV).

This isn't God shaming or strong-arming you into honor through his Word. He's a good Father, and that's just not his modus operandi. But this passage sets a precedent that bestowing honor is what you're *meant* to do as his image-bearer.

Same goes with grace (7:47).

And forgiveness (11:4).

And even money (Deuteronomy 16:16–17).

As vessels of honor, we never show up empty-handed, because we've been filled to overflowing by our Father's kingdom reserve. Throughout your life, you will receive countless invitations to come up higher—to let go and lean into God's best when it comes to honor. This will most certainly require an upside-down kingdom perspective when walking in honor within the body of Christ:

- *We bestow honor and dignity on every last one of the least of these.* "Those members of the body which we think to be less honorable, on these we bestow greater honor" (1 Corinthians 12:23).
- *We allocate greater measures of honor and covering where they're needed.* "Our unpresentable parts have greater modesty, but our presentable parts have no need" (vv. 23–24).
- *We outdo one another in honor for the good of the body of Christ and for the sake of unity.* "God composed the body, having given greater honor to that part which lacks it, that there should be no schism in the body, but that the members should have the same care for one another. And if one member suffers, all the

> members suffer with it; or if one member is honored, all the members rejoice with it. Now you are the body of Christ, and members individually" (vv. 24–27).

From a purely human standpoint, these honor directives sound like madness. Westernized American culture implores you to embrace a postmodern, individualistic mindset that screams, *Take it all! Quick, before someone else does!*

This scarcity mentality keeps you poor in spirit and stuck in your current position. But Christ not only implores but empowers you to do exactly the opposite: *Give it all! Quick, before someone else does!*

This abundance mentality never shames you. Instead, it encourages you to actively participate in what God is doing. It prompts you to honor apostles, prophets, teachers, pastors, and evangelists at all levels—seers, discerners, and administrators alike—knowing their success is quite literally your success. We are one body of believers, and we need one another. I need you, you need me, and we all need the gifts God uniquely bestows on his children in honor. We are uniquely gifted but collectively unstoppable when we let the Lord guide us into deeper and deeper levels of honor in the church and in the world.

Taking the high road of honor will require more and more from season to season, and it's up to us to be sensitive to the Lord beckoning us upward. He calls, and we must answer. Honor yourself for who you are as an image-bearer and what you carry as the Lord's vessel. Then honor others as you would yourself. In doing this, you give all glory and honor to God—the only one who is truly worthy of honor in his own right.

Honorable Reflections

What makes you a vessel of honor?

Are you comparing yourself with others or being the best you can be?

How are you honoring yourself right now, in this current season, the way God is calling you to do?

How can you better honor yourself in order to better honor others?

7

Honoring the Anointing

But the anointing which you have received from Him abides in you, and you do not need that anyone teach you; but as the same anointing teaches you concerning all things, and is true, and is not a lie, and just as it has taught you, you will abide in Him.

1 John 2:27 NKJV

Now, what we want is a fresh supply, a fresh anointing and fresh power, and if we seek it, and seek it with all our hearts, we will obtain it.

Dwight L. Moody

We don't know each other by the flesh but by the Spirit (2 Corinthians 5:16). Humankind doesn't know Jesus by the flesh anymore either, but by his Spirit living in us. We are walking, talking, living, breathing, new creations—co-raised with Christ and dead to our former selves. We have been restored to our original identity as image-bearers of our creator God. Our unique reflections of his multifaceted character manifest in a multitude of anointings in our lives. These anointings augment our basic identity as his image-bearers and make us truly special in the eyes of God and man. Discerning who someone is beyond his or her baseline identity is the first step to honoring the anointing on that person's life.

Now, everyone has different graces and anointings on their lives that flow from *the* Anointing—the Holy Spirit. No matter who we are, what we've done, or where we've been, we are now new creations like Christ himself. Although our Messiah is timeless and will forever be the beginning and the end, he also resurrected in a new incarnate form. He continues to manifest new facets of who he is, and in him we carry what is known as the *Christos* anointing. The word *Christos* means "the Messiah" or the "anointed" One.[19] *Christos* is derived from the Greek word *chriō*, meaning "the idea of contact; to smear or rub."[20] To be anointed is far more than getting a delighted pat on the head from your heavenly Father or some kind of a high five from Jesus. Your Creator literally *smears* the essence of himself into your very being, infusing his own anointing into yours. Why? So that even in the flesh, you can do things the flesh cannot do (2 Corinthians 4:7).

Now, you're not God. You're not the Messiah, the anointed One. But if you are *in* Christ, you *are* one with your Creator. Far more than a formal title or an earthly expression of intimacy, the *Christos* anointing is a representation of your union with God in Christ by the power of the Holy Spirit. The *Christos* anointing is the highest possible honor a believer can receive from a holy God.

Interestingly, some teachers don't believe there are different types of anointings beyond the *Christos* anointing. I respectfully disagree and believe that the Holy Spirit can accomplish vastly different purposes in and through God's people with them. Healing anointings, prophetic anointings, and deliverance anointings are just a handful of the ways the Spirit commissions and qualifies us for his good works. None of us were created to carry every anointing, but together as the body of Christ, we represent our Father's character in full, bearing a clearer image of our Creator.

The anointings we carry don't replace or compete with the *Christos* anointing; they flow like a mountain spring from the Holy Spirit living in us. Think of the Holy Spirit as fuel in a vehicle—absolutely necessary for movement and operation yet not the vehicle itself. It's what *mobilizes* the vehicle. We are like different anointing vehicles all fueled by the Holy Spirit. The more quickly we can discern what kind of vehicle a person is, the quicker we can honor it in them. People of all ages and stages—even little children—can carry anointings without knowing it. And it's up to us to perceive their anointing, call it out in them, and call it forth through them, allowing them to shine so brightly that we can collectively bask in their glory glow.

Honoring the anointing in people can take patience, since not all people carry their anointing as a dominant feature. Simply put, all people are anointed, but not all people walk in their anointing. At least not yet. Anointed people are often skittish yet confident—insecure in the natural world yet secure in God. The more we honor people's anointing in the midst of their humanity, the more grace we will receive from God.

God will do nothing on the earth unless he first gives it to his prophets. It takes maturity to honor the anointing in others, and that maturity is present only in high-level spiritual kings or queens. We must see others from a kingdom perspective rather than through the low-level filter of an orphan spirit. This enables us to decipher the best in people. When we're unable or unwilling to see, acknowledge, and honor the anointing in others, it causes people to depreciate in perceived honor and value. By choosing first to observe in curiosity rather than assume in cynicism and second to steward, protect, and mine for hidden treasure even in the most unlikely vessels, we will enable people to discover who they really are and what unique anointing they really carry in Christ.

Catching the Anointing

Here's the best part: Honoring the anointing in others will help you discover and receive the fullness of your own anointing. When you honor someone's anointing and allow that person to shine brightly, you position yourself to receive and sometimes even "catch" the anointing from him or her. Honor those who faithfully steward finances, and you'll find yourself doing the same. Honor those who move in signs and wonders, and you'll find yourself doing the same. The grace given to generals of the faith can come onto you when you stay in proximity to see them, serve them, and sow into them. Whatever you need to do to be in the room, do it! Pay the price. Shut your mouth. Put them first. Serve and sow. Make yourself available. The honor will come back to you in a harvest either immediately or incrementally.

Here's the best part: honoring the anointing in others will help you discover and receive the fullness of your own anointing.

Anointings are contagious in the best kind of way. But it's important to remember that while you can catch an anointing, you can also catch a disease. As an image-bearer, you bear the image of what you behold. And if you're beholding someone or something that is not God-honoring, you'll catch whatever that person or thing carries. Be aware of what and whom you allow into your life.

Catching the anointing is not about praying a particular prayer or walking through a series of steps to get anointed. The very act of seeking an anointing for selfish ambition will keep you far from it. Catching the anointing is about honoring the anointing in others *first* and joyfully embracing the reality of your oneness with them in Christ. All they have is yours, and all you have is theirs. There is no scarcity in our Father's kingdom, only abundance. Anointings are not finite resources; they're renewable and transferable. Honor begets honor, after all. And honor translates best in the overflow of God's grace.

Growing up Christian

In some cases, growing up in a Christian home can be a huge deterrent to honor because of the hypocrisies, fake religious tendencies, and masterful cover-ups of putting on and off church personas and masks for self-gratifying convenience. Don't misunderstand me. I certainly see the value of faith being intricately woven into all aspects of home, family, and community life. Being raised in an authentic honor culture is the highest privilege a child can have. I certainly don't resent my own Christian upbringing. As flawed as my homelife was at times, Christ was presented to me from an early age, and following him was part of our culture. It's just what we did in our family. But I know this to be true: I took my Christian upbringing for granted.

I was beyond privileged as a young man, spiritually stuck-up, and wholly unappreciative of the sacrifices made for me by my family, my church, and even my God. As evidenced by my teenage double life, I knew how to straddle the line between the secular and the sacred all too comfortably. I professed Jesus with my lips, but I became my own little god in my heart and mind, running from and rebelling against both my earthly father and my heavenly Father. After years front row and center in my dad's pew, I knew just about everything there was to know *about* God—but I didn't actually know *him* at all. And I know I'm not the only ungrateful little lamb whom Jesus has had to run after and bring back home into the fold.

Growing up within the confines of a family ministry and stepping into itinerant ministry at a very young age, I've gotten to know the good, the bad, and the ugly of the man-made church. I can honestly say that I've seen it all—or at least I know someone who has. I'm connected to generals of the faith who have lived through the worst of the worst in Christendom—corrupt televangelism, prosperity gospel manipulations, lies, deceit, misogyny, abuse—you name it. It's no wonder so many believers are now walking through a deconstruction process, dissecting their own Christian upbringing, and questioning the validity of the church, organized religion, and in some cases even Christ himself.

As a collective body, we've gone soft on bad behavior in the name of false honor. And when the offenses boil out of control, we blast leaders by name with slanderous open letter corrections on social media—all in the name of fans, followers, and other vanity metrics. Zero accountability. No moral compass. Far too few Christlike examples for the flock to emulate. In a digital age, dishonor spreads like a disease when we surrender to the decaying adage "It's just how we've always done things." Spreading and spewing dishonor, gossip, and slander publicly, even virally, is what our old carnal nature has always done! With social media, this has become even more of a pandemic. It's up to our generation to reclaim and restore honor in this context.

The answer to these complex, systemic, generational issues within the church is simple: adhere to Jesus' teachings on church discipline in Matthew 18. I've seen so many believers pick and choose which parts of the clear biblical protocol they *want* to follow. Then they throw out the rest. When we do this, we set a graceless precedent that proves church isn't really a safe, loving, honor-filled place after all. We can—and must—do better than this. So let's break down Christ's teaching line by line:

> ***Step 1:*** "Moreover if your brother sins against you, go and tell him his fault between you and him alone. If he hears you, you have gained your brother" (v. 15 NKJV).
>
> We're not only meant to lovingly confront the offenses of our brothers and sisters; we're meant to do it confidentially (if possible) and only from a place of authentic relationship. This preserves the offender's privacy and gives him or her a genuine opportunity to repent without creating cause for broader corporate offense. This kind, compassionate approach can demonstrate honor in a profound way, proving that you value the anointing your brother or sister carries even more than the struggle he or she is currently dealing with. You value it so much, in fact, that you can't continue allowing the person to operate in a way that's not becoming of that anointing. If that person can receive your loving correction, he or she will trust you for life.

Step 2: "But if he will not hear, take with you one or two more, that 'by the mouth of two or three witnesses every word may be established'" (v. 16).

Sometimes our first attempts at loving correction can go unreceived, especially when someone believes his or her honor is being called into question. Instead of writing these people off or backing down on truth, muster the courage to go to Step 2. Find another brother or sister who can mediate the conversation, affirm biblical truth, and help preserve the relationship through healthy conflict. This third party (or parties) will listen more than talk, having ideally little to no vested personal interest in the matter, so an unbiased biblical position can be maintained. This stage in the process must never become a combative, accusatory calling onto the carpet. Instead, you and one or two other believers must approach the offender in love and with a goal of calling him or her to repentance. This preserves honor and holds the person to a standard that is holy and pleasing to God. No personal agendas. Period.

Step 3: "And if he refuses to hear them, tell it to the church. But if he refuses even to hear the church, let him be to you like a heathen and a tax collector" (v. 17).

This third step is perhaps one of the most misunderstood passages in all of Scripture. Yes, there will be offenders who don't listen to reason,

> and this stubbornness creates a lack of safety within a culture of honor. A church can't stand for this, and if we do, we're not really a church at all. Yet many churchgoing types weaponize this passage with a perceived license to gossip, slander, shame, and condemn offenders publicly—even from the pulpit! Manipulative witch hunts never lead offenders to true and lasting repentance. Kindness does (Romans 2:4). If you've exhausted every other biblical option and it *really* comes to telling the church—which can, in fact, be a small group of elders—the end goal must not be an ultimatum or excommunication but redemption and restoration.

If you let this spirit of honor be in you and people still won't listen, then you have permission to treat them the way Jesus treated heathens and tax collectors: with a reckless love that honors their anointing even as they sin.

Honoring Victims and Offenders

It's important to note that covering a believer in order to honor his or her anointing does not mean "covering up" the sins of predators within a culture of abuse. Cover-ups cannot exist within a culture of honor. Jesus gave us church-discipline rules of engagement in Matthew 18 so we can create safe, productive spaces for healing and restoration for those who have been hurt by the church and those who have fallen from grace. Can abuse ever be tolerated in the body of Christ? Of course not. Are there consequences for actions? Of course. There *must* be.

Yet there must be equal opportunities for redemption and restoration of both prisoners and captors alike—yes, victims *and* offenders. Jesus didn't just forgive sinners; he left them changed forever by his grace. When we collectively commit to living out an iron-sharpens-iron existence in our faith communities, we can cultivate and preserve a culture of honor. After outlining the three steps we just looked at, Jesus added this:

> "Assuredly, I say to you, whatever you bind on earth will be bound in heaven, and whatever you loose on earth will be loosed in heaven. Again I say to you that if two of you agree on earth concerning anything that they ask, it will be done for them by My Father in heaven. For where two or three are gathered together in My name, I am there in the midst of them." (Matthew 18:18–20 NKJV)

Whatever the outcome of your Matthew 18 activities, take great care to bestow honor publicly no matter what. Alleged offenders are innocent until proven guilty. And even when they are proven guilty, we must be willing to treat them with dignity and respect in public. Speak kindly, lovingly, and restoratively of them and to them, believing that God can work a redemptive miracle in their lives. Resist the urge to define offenders permanently by their offense. Labels like *predator*, *abuser*, *gossip*, *thief*, and even *sinner* only affirm the antichrist spirit seeking to own people's identity. Honor offenders as you would victims, because they absolutely have been victimized, manipulated, and exploited by the violent persona of sin himself, Satan.

Honoring Your Own Anointing

If you want to live out an iron-sharpens-iron faith in community, you must first *be* iron. We cannot give away what we do not yet have (Matthew 10:8). We cannot glorify God with our bodies unless we acknowledge the holy temples that they are (1 Corinthians 6:19–20). And we cannot love our neighbor as ourselves until we first learn to love ourselves rightly (Mark 12:31). This comes not through vain ambition, self-promotion, or status-seeking ladder-climbing. Nor does it come by self-loathing, penance payments, or codependence. Being iron comes by acknowledging, receiving, and honoring the anointing on your own life and carrying that anointing in obedience to the Lord.

Everybody has an anointing. Yes, even you. As human as you are, you can still honor yourself—the vessel God has chosen—to carry out his call on your life. God honored you with an anointing in your humanity so that you would walk it out in his strength, not your own. If you can't honor the anointing on your own life, how can you ever honor the anointing on anyone else?

Take a cue from our friend Elisha, who honored the anointing on the prophet Elijah to the point of being a bit of a nuisance. It's unclear exactly how long Elisha served Elijah before he became his successor, but clearly the two had a strong bond. Elijah told Elisha not once, not twice, but three times to stay behind so he could travel to another place (2 Kings 2:1–18). Elijah would eventually be taken from Elisha; this they both already knew. Elisha adamantly refused his master's dismissal and stayed close by to continue serving and honoring this man of God.

At first glance, you might see Elisha's defiance as dishonoring: he disobeyed the direct and repeated command of his master to stay behind. Look more closely, and you might see Elisha passing a true test of discipleship—proving that he would never leave his master willingly, under any circumstances. Whether Elijah was annoyed, delighted, or perplexed by this, he ascended into heaven when God called him—and his mantle (garment) descended to Elisha's open and willing spirit. Elisha received the "double portion" he had asked his master for (vv. 9–11). He took up Elijah's mantle and became the Lord's leading prophet in the land, parting rivers, bringing miracles, and so much more.

Elisha honored the prophetic anointing on Elijah's life, but he also honored the anointing on his own life as well—to be Elijah's successor, carrying forth his legacy and doing even greater things than his master before him. And it wasn't in spite of his master; it was because of the firm foundation Elijah had laid in Elisha's life. There will come a time for a leadership mantle to be assumed in your own life. Resist the urge to craft your own garment based on trends or preferences. Receive the mantle of your predecessors—yes, even the elders you occasionally struggle to honor—and assume the double portion of honor that can become manifest in your generation. (More to come on that in chapter 8.)

A double portion of anything is a key theme in Scripture, one we're often hesitant to acknowledge and receive. Elisha received a double portion of Elijah's spirit, even after being defiant by definition. Hannah received a double portion from her husband, even when she couldn't bear children (1 Samuel 1:1–5). Job received back double what he had before his time of suffering (Job 42:10–17). Depending on the circumstances, Scripture promises us a double portion of blessing or a double portion of judgment (Isaiah 61:7; Revelation 18:6).

> ***One thing is certain: when you honor the anointing, a double portion of honor is your rightful inheritance.***

One thing is certain: When you honor the anointing, a double portion of honor is your rightful inheritance. It's yours for the taking. Will you acknowledge, receive, and honor the anointing on your own life? Will you honor the anointing on the lives of others, even when it gets difficult? Will you accomplish what your predecessors couldn't—or wouldn't—by honoring the anointing in *all* believers? You wouldn't be the first. But you'd be the exception. Be the exception.

Honoring Through Availability

If you want to catch an anointing, you not only need to be around; you need to be available. Proximity is critical, but you must be ready and eager to serve and sow. Like a major league baseball outfielder, you can't stand firm in center field and expect the ball to come to you! You not only have to go get it; you have to do something with it. Honoring through availability means you must be humble, hungry, and flexible enough to pivot when the prophet's mantle falls in unexpected places.

Whether you grew up in a Christian home or not, you likely heard the story of Noah's ark for the first time in childhood. Whether it was taught to you in biblically semi-accurate flannelgraph format or presented as a religious myth held by orthodox Christian, Jewish, Islamic, and other Abrahamic traditions, the story widely depicts Noah as a righteous man who either saved or condemned the world by God's own hand (depending on which commentators you ask).

Son of Lamech in the godly line of Seth (versus the ungodly line of Cain), Noah came along only about ten generations after his great-great-greats, Adam and Eve. The world was still young, with most of humankind still tripping its way through deep-seated generational sin. We had embraced a broken, sinner identity—a way of "wickedness" with nothing but evil thoughts (Genesis 6:5). Scripture says we were so wicked, in fact, that our Creator actually regretted creating us and had in mind to wipe us out (vv. 6–7). Yes, really. But Noah, whose name aptly means "relief," found favor in the eyes of God. He was also blameless in the eyes of man and walked with God on the daily, worthy of honor on all counts. Noah's rare obedience gave the Lord renewed hope in humankind. Instead of hitting a full-on divine reset on our species, God decided to extend grace and favor to Noah's entire family (his wife, his three sons, and their wives) by putting them to work on a grand kingdom project. You know how the story goes:

Hey, Noah,
Storm's coming. Build an ark. Gather the animals.
Dove's on its way.
See you in forty days.
Love you,
God

Sure, there's a lot more to it than that. But all we really need to understand about Noah is that other than asking a few clarifying questions, he didn't hesitate to obey the Lord's command. Motivated by fear of a flood, fear of the Lord, or perhaps a little bit of both, he got to work building a triple-decker, ocean-worthy ark…*nowhere near a body of water.* He looked like a fool to the heathens around him, the ones he continually called to repentance (v. 5; 1 Peter 3:18–20). Noah didn't exactly offer anyone a ticket to ride on the ark with his family when the flood came, but he invited people into a repentance that might have prevented the flood completely if the people had only listened to God's prophet and obeyed. But I digress.

Noah was not only obedient to the Lord; he also made himself available to God. He honored God's time and his own, giving the Lord every single kind of firstfruit—time, energy, and likely even money. (Somebody had to pay for all that lumber, right?) He did everything God asked and nothing he didn't. And God's plan to cleanse the earth of wickedness was put into action, pointing ultimately to the defeat of sin in the coming Christ. Noah was a prophet with a heavy mantle—one his three sons all wanted to catch.

Three cheers for Noah, am I right? *Clap! Clap! Clap!*

Oh, that we might be used like this faithful servant, this willing vessel, this honorable man of God who was…*passed out drunk and naked* in a tent one chapter later (Genesis 9:20–27)! *Seriously?*

Ask ten Bible scholars why Noah got drunk, and they'll give you ten different speculations, most of them steeped in shame. Truth is, Scripture doesn't say why. While some are adamant that even God can't take the sin out of our sinful nature, others make excuses for Noah—saying the ole lightweight probably got drunk by accident because of his old age, or perhaps his "inexperience" with the sheer abundance of running God's first vineyard.

Even if Noah deliberately tried to dull the trauma of being tasked to condemn the world by faith (Hebrews 11:7), it's hard not to identify with this righteous man's unrighteousness. I'm sure many of us would struggle to stay sober-minded in the aftermath of something like that.

Understanding Noah's trauma doesn't excuse his behavior, though. Ephesians 5:18 is clear that we are not to be drunk on wine but on the Holy Spirit. But Noah's behavior isn't really the point of this scriptural account. Understanding the cost of his obedience is what moved two of his three sons to "cover" their father's shame in his struggle:

> And Noah began to be a farmer, and he planted a vineyard. Then he drank of the wine and was drunk, and became uncovered in his tent. And Ham, the father of Canaan, saw the nakedness of his father, and told his two brothers outside. But Shem and Japheth took a garment, laid it on both their shoulders, and went backward and covered the nakedness of their father. Their faces were turned away, and they did not see their father's nakedness. (Genesis 9:20–23)

It's important to note that when Shem and Japheth covered their father, they weren't "covering up" his sin. I mean, the full account is right there in Genesis 9 for the generations to read for all eternity (thank you very much, Moses). Granted, this little post-flood family didn't yet have the teachings of Jesus in Matthew 18 so they could follow appropriate protocol for such an offense. Yet instead of gossiping and pointing out their father's weakness, as Ham did, Shem and Japheth instinctively honored the anointing on their father's life—in the midst of his abject humanity. They couldn't change history. They couldn't pretend the incident never happened. But they could honor their father for who he really was—his Creator's image-bearer who probably took his eyes off the prize for a split second.

What's more, Shem and Japheth affirmed Noah's heavy mantle and made themselves available to honor their father—and thereby catch his mantle, his anointing, and his blessing. This is what it means to *cover* your leaders, to honor them and help them avoid shame that would detract from the call of God on their life.

The next morning must have been awkward at Noah's breakfast table. Dad all hungover, likely getting the story secondhand from his wife or another family member. Scripture doesn't say whether Shem and Japheth called him out in love or not, but it does say how much Noah appreciated them choosing to honor the anointing on his life. He richly blessed them because they were available for him—ready to serve, support, and love Noah even when he couldn't rightly love himself. He said of them afterward, "Blessed be the Lord, the God of Shem, and may Canaan be his servant. May God enlarge Japheth, and may he dwell in the tents of Shem; and may Canaan be his servant" (Genesis 9:26–27).

I'd be remiss if I didn't teach about the painful reality that existed for the other brother, Ham, that same morning. Although Noah blessed the two sons who covered him, he cursed his third—not Ham himself, but Ham's descendants, the Canaanites: "So Noah awoke from his wine, and knew what his younger son had done to him. Then he said: 'Cursed be Canaan; a servant of servants he shall be to his brethren'" (vv. 24–25).

If you think this curse a little harsh for one passing act of dishonor, consider Ham's alleged track record according to the Babylonian Talmud: Castration. Incest. Homosexuality. Rape. Scandal![21] Ham was *not* a righteous dude. Sure, he was in *proximity* to Noah—close enough to tear him down and try to *take* his mantle through demonic levels of dishonor. Whether Ham dishonoring his father in Genesis 9 was a "simple" poking of fun or something far worse, Noah cursed Ham's family line—a line that would eventually be redeemed through biblical heroes like Rahab the prostitute and Tamar, princess of Israel.

Bottom line? Your decision to honor the anointing in others or not—especially when they are at their worst—will determine the level of honor you will receive. We honor the anointing on others' lives simply because it honors God to do so. Refusing to do so dishonors God, as well as the person you dishonor. Will you be like Ham, slanderous and shaming, or like Shem and Japheth, honoring and kind? As a biological or spiritual parent, which kinds of kids would you prefer to have?

My own spiritual father, Pastor Benny Hinn, is oh-so-easy to honor. The way he carries himself as a man of God practically demands that I lavish him with everything I have out of the overflow of my heart. He gets my trust, my time, my talent, and even my tithe—and I am privileged to bask in the overflow of honor he carries. But the true tests come when we honor people who aren't so easy to honor—leaders gone astray, well-meaning saints turned to sin. There is a time for separation in the flock. Even Paul and Barnabas parted ways, and they were better for it. But staying available to honor the gold in people no matter what? This is the essence of honoring the anointing.

Perhaps you are uniquely anointed to call people higher—to elevate a particular conversation or bring about tangible behavioral reform in the church universal. Perhaps you are meant to live a life worthy of honor and emulation. Perhaps you are meant to reclaim the lost art of honor in your generation, blessing your biological and spiritual lineage for generations to come. I am believing this for you, in Jesus' name!

Honorable Reflections

Is it possible to separate the "human side" from the "anointed office" of the man or woman of God?

How do you honor the anointing on someone's life, even in his or her humanity?

What's the difference between covering someone and covering up sin?

What could be the generational impacts of honoring the anointing on someone?

8

Double Honor

Let the elders who rule well be considered worthy of double honor, especially those who labor in preaching and teaching. For the Scripture says, "You shall not muzzle an ox when it treads out the grain," and, "The laborer deserves his wages."

1 Timothy 5:17–18

The mind is a wonderful tool, but a terrible master. Sometimes what God is doing will offend the mind, but the spirit will be able to discern His presence.

Bill Johnson

Anointings are nothing new. They're ancient, given by God to fathers of the faith and passed down through the generations like flaming Olympic torches. Receiving this inheritance—these precious generational heirlooms of honor—requires you to be in proximity in mind, body, and spirit to those who carry the anointing you are destined to catch and multiply.

Consider again our friend Elisha. He was only able to catch the mantle of Elijah because it fell off the ascending prophet right next to him (2 Kings 2:13–14). If you want the honor anointing—in

Elisha's case, a double portion of Elijah's spirit—you have to be close enough to your predecessors to allow the grace to come upon you. This is why the growing generational gap in the church of Jesus Christ is such a huge problem. We refuse to embrace our oneness in Christ, and we become increasingly distant from and disillusioned with one another. And yet, like Elijah's mantle, parts of our kingdom inheritance are only available through generational revelation, meaning you can only "catch it" by honoring the vessels of old and tapping into a glory that transcends the ages.

Honor is always passed down, always transcendent. And yet, generation after generation, we fail to pass the torch. Elder generations assume that the younger generation lost it, and younger generations assume that the elder generation never tried to pass it down in the first place. Regardless, the anointing must be passed on in order to be multiplied. Whether we're on the giving or receiving end of the honor anointing, we must be willing to take responsibility and step into place for the glorious transfer. We must make it our own by humbly submitting ourselves to the due process of the Lord.

Like Elisha, when we honor those who went before us who were able to receive a portion of an anointing, we can receive the fullness of that mantle and God can double it. This double honor only comes to those who are willing to honor their preceding prophets no matter the cost. You can't *snatch* an anointing—you must *catch* it. And to catch the flaming torch, you must be present, purposeful, and in proximity.

Like Elijah, when we honor the pure-gold potential in those we are called to lead—even when they disobey us, annoy us, and don't do things the way we think they should—we can willingly impart the anointings we carry and God will double our protégés' anointings. You can't cling to your mantle too tightly, and you can't carelessly shirk your responsibilities, dropping the torch and muttering about how you've "done your time." You must make every effort to honorably bestow the anointing on the next generation, believing in faith that they will do even greater things with it than you ever could (or would).

When both the giving and receiving parties take responsibility for and authority in their part of the transition, both parties end up being served, empowered, and honored in the process. Whether our elders need support in releasing, our emerging leaders need support in receiving, or both, the honor anointing must be passed—and doubled.

It's inexcusable to let the anointing get lost in transition. God's strategy is that this inheritance be passed down as part of a kingdom legacy. Who are we to say otherwise? So elders, accept responsibility for releasing your portion—even when emerging leaders don't seem ready, willing, or able to receive. Emerging leaders, accept responsibility for receiving and doubling your elders' portion—even if they haven't done a great job of demonstrating how. Step into the authority God gave you and meet your honor counterpart right where he or she is, with compassion. Seek to understand, not to be understood, and find the way forward together.

When Honor Turns Deadly

Anointings are precious and powerful. Rightly wielded, they will shake nations and make history as they are multiplied through the generations. We must be willing to go low in honor, humility, and purity of spirit in order to receive a double portion. But if honor isn't flowing from a pure place, a double portion of anything can turn deadly.

If honor isn't flowing from a pure place, a double portion of anything can turn deadly.

Consider Samson, a long-locked Nazarite judge with superhuman strength who was called to help free the Israelites from captivity. Samson's multiplication of strength came with some spiritual strings attached. Not only could Samson not partake of any alcohol or unclean foods, but his once-barren mother couldn't either while she was pregnant with him (Judges 13:2–5). She passed a torch of ritual cleanliness on to her infant son, and God blessed him as he grew tall, strong, and handsome.

Samson kept his hair long as a symbol of his covenant of strength in the Lord. But beyond that, he broke about every rule in the book. He ate a honeycomb out of the dead carcass of a lion (14:8–9). He served alcohol at his weeklong wedding reception to a forbidden bride and murdered thirty Philistines over a riddle (vv. 1–3, 10–20). Finally, his sordid affair with Delilah, a Philistine, cost him his seven braided locks of hair—not to mention his strength, his eyes, his freedom, and eventually his life (Judges 16).

Now, Samson's elders within the children of Israel hadn't exactly walked out their anointings honorably either. Scripture says that generation after generation, they were just plain evil. So God continued to deliver them into the hands of the Philistines for forty years (13:1). Samson followed suit, time and again shirking the call on his life. But ironically, Samson's comparatively short twenty-year season as a less-than-righteous judge wasn't a complete failure. He took out more than three thousand of his enemies in his own death (Judges 16).

Samson clearly didn't honor the strength anointing on his own life. After Samson was humbled, God permitted him to reclaim his anointing, but he didn't live to see the fruits of a double-honor life. Friend, we were meant for more than this.

Offended by the Vessel

Even when our elders haven't received their own mantles in full, we must be willing to go after generational anointings and steward them in increasingly faithful measures. This is the essence of double honor. This means we must esteem our elders, empowering and enabling them to pass the torch. Whether they handle the handoff with care and compassion, stumble and drop it so you have to pick it up, or deliberately throw it out of your way, it's up to you to meet them where they are. No more shaming and blaming. You have the authority to carry the torch forward. Even when you don't agree with your elders, you can show them that you understand, appreciate, and honor their perspective. Even if you have to catch the torch as they drop it, you must carry it forward. This is the way of double honor.

Ironically, millennials and Gen Zers don't struggle with this notion as much as Generation X. Unlike their baby boomer parents, Gen Xers are notoriously quick to dismiss their imperfect elders, convinced they themselves could do it better if the old guard would just get out of the way. Instead of receiving a mantle, they let pride and offense get in the way.

When we take that attitude, we light our own torches and carry them forward, pretending they were God's anointing all along. I dare say this is why the generational religious gap exists in America, with 84 percent of the Greatest Generation, 76 percent of baby boomers, 67 percent of Generation Xers, and only 49 percent of millennials identifying as Christian. The result? Across the generations, fewer than 50 percent of Americans practice their faith by attending religious services weekly or more, making 50 percent of people straight-up out of proximity to catch any kind of anointing.[22] When we carry a torch that God didn't light? We're destined to quench the fire, not fan the flame of the Spirit.

Interestingly, millennials and Gen Zers are poised and ready to pick up slack in the body of Christ. Many of us were coddled and sheltered from responsibility for most of our childhood, and our proverbial plates are ready to be filled! Why is it that nobody thinks we'd be willing to carry the torch? We're open! Granted, we might not carry it the way our honorable elders want us to, but we will carry it forward. Friend, we must be willing to meet people where they are. Keep honoring people, whether they're young and you're older or you're older and they're young. Resist the temptation to be offended by the vessel. God uses our idiosyncrasies to pass down new graces with new mantles. And God might offend the mind to get to a heart. This means that he will break the boxes of our small mindsets to open up glorious and life-transforming encounters in our psyches, emotions, and entire beings!

Speaking of offensive vessels…many people are offended by me, at least at first. How I look, how I talk, and how I act in boldness are unusual in most church cultures—probably about as unusual as John the Baptist's hemp-wearing, locust-eating ways were back in the day. Why are they so offended by me as a vessel? Religiosity? Ignorance? Envy? God only knows. As humans, we gravitate to what we understand because it makes us feel safe. And when we don't feel safe, we reject what we should honor because of our issues, not other people's. When our understanding is challenged, we either get spiritually hungry or get defensive. God can work with either, but the hungry, open, and willing ones are usually far better positioned to receive.

If we can honor people at their worst, we can help bring out their best. No shaming, no blaming, no finger-pointing.

Oh, they didn't hand me the torch nicely and with a smile.

Come on.

Oh, they fell and dropped their torch, so I don't want to be affiliated with that.

Enough already.

Oh, they weren't where they said they'd be to give me the torch, so I went home.

No excuses.

Honor other people. Meet them where they are, and you will position yourself to receive a double portion of their anointing.

A sense of entitlement says, *Well, I did my part, so it's on them.* If any stronghold may be broken off your spirit by reading this book, may it be this one. Reclaiming something that's been lost, especially honor, will require you to go above and beyond when it comes to unity. Our elders cannot succeed in releasing the anointing without us. We cannot succeed in receiving the anointing without them. Like the hand and the eye, we not only need one another, we are one body! We carry unique anointings, but in the Spirit, there is no you versus me. There is no young versus old. There is no us versus them. We are all one, and it's a seamless flow of honor we are meant to carry forward.

Every time I've come up against generational gaps in the church, I'm astonished to see how easy it is to compromise in this area. Our aging fathers are still dealing with King Saul-level insecurities, while our young Davids remain either apathetic and aloof or entitled and estranged. When good King Solomon's rebellious son Rehoboam promised his elders, "My little finger shall be thicker than my father's waist," it wasn't spoken as a blessing of double honor but as a generational curse (1 Kings 12:10–11) that we are now uniquely anointed to break in Christ (Ezekiel 18:20; Galatians 3:13). Not only do we have the opportunity to be like our heavenly Father, who constantly gives us such scandalously undeserved grace, but we also can break the generational curse and cycles of bondage, anger, and death by moving in the grace of the gospel of Jesus Christ. It's up to us to lighten the burden on the body of Christ. If not us, who? If not now, when?

On this day of visitation, Christ is inviting you to be his habitation. Yours isn't the first generation to be invited. Jesus lamented deeply over Jerusalem's rejection of him and of his prophets:

> "O Jerusalem, Jerusalem, the one who kills the prophets and stones those who are sent to her! How often I wanted to gather your children together, as a hen gathers her brood under her wings, but you were not willing! See! Your house is left to you desolate; and assuredly, I say to you, you shall not see Me until the time comes when you say, 'Blessed is He who comes in the name of the Lord!'" (Luke 13:34–35)

So many of us dishonor and even demonize the people and the anointings of God simply because we don't understand them. This was the mistake of Jerusalem. Much of what God wants to bless us with will require us to get out of our own way, our own thought processes, and our own prefabricated religious boxes. When we stay spiritually hungry and bestow honor, we will be able to receive the hidden secret gifts and go to the next level with God.

Many people in the church don't ascend to these new levels because they refuse to progress from a mindset of visitation to one of habitation. Sometimes when I attend a meeting, their defenses are already up: *Okay, kid, show us what you've got!* They see me as a punk kid who had better perform if I want to be treated as a prophet. These arrogant Pharisees carry the sourest countenances (I sometimes call them "fart faces") because they are manifesting sulfur-and-brimstone demons. They try to test or contest me in the spirit, tainting the atmosphere with their unbelief and dishonor. I know the Bible says to test the spirits, but we are meant to do so in honor nonetheless. Jesus limited his miraculous demonstrations in his home country. His power wasn't limited, but the honor there certainly was (Mark 6:4–5). There was a values misalignment.

Religious scholar D. E. Hiebert describes this values misalignment in his book *The Gospel of Mark*: "[Jesus] felt it morally impossible to exercise his beneficent power in their behalf in the face of their unbelief (Matthew 13:58). It closed the door against the operation of His power. He refused to force Himself upon those who did not want Him."[23]

In his earlier commentary on Mark's gospel, scholar James Brooks explains the human element in the supernatural this way: "God and his Son could do anything, but they have chosen to limit themselves in accordance with human response…Jesus was not the kind of miracle worker whose primary purpose was to impress his viewers [with no regard to the nature of their disposition]."[24]

What if we could be different from the people in Jesus' hometown? What would happen if we had honor in our hearts? What if we didn't require evidence *before* the miracles but positioned our hearts expectantly for God to move in and through his prophets? What if we let go of a critical and cynical skeptic spirit and embraced a curiosity and hunger that could lead to breakthrough? *Miracles! Signs and wonders! The glory of God would break out!* Honor brings the very best out of a vessel and enables us to live in the double-honor reality of the gospel.

Coming against a spirit of dishonor is one of the things that gets me into trouble the most. When I'm ministering to a group of hungry ones, hours feel like mere minutes as we embrace the Spirit. But when I'm ministering to a crowd of critical cynics, minutes feel like hours as we combat a spirit of skepticism. I'll be honest with you: Life is short, and I don't have time for this. When I encounter a skeptic spirit, the Lord almost always leads me to call it out on boldness. Using Jesus' words to the Pharisees, I let the hypocrites have it: "Woe to you, scribes and Pharisees, hypocrites! For you are like whitewashed tombs which indeed appear beautiful outwardly, but inside are full of dead men's bones and all uncleanness" (Matthew 23:27).

Admittedly, this high-challenge approach occasionally closes church doors to me. Hypocrites rarely enjoy being called out, especially in public. It's uncomfortable. It's humbling. It's intensely stretching. But it's *necessary*. Sometimes honor looks like speaking truth in love—because it's the only honorable thing one can do. And I'll keep pressing on that trigger until something shifts.

Jesus wasn't afraid to flip tables, and neither am I. Sometimes that's what love looks like. This takes sensitivity, wisdom, and maturity, I'm aware, but it's also just an integral part of the anointing on my life. You won't always learn in seminary or ministry school to calibrate invitation and challenge the way Jesus did. No three-point-sermon training can equip you for this kind of hands-on good work. Only the Holy Spirit can school you on challenging the barriers to honor being bestowed in either direction.

When the Lord leads me to challenge a skeptic spirit within a house or worship, I must always be ready to shake the dust off and move on (Matthew 10:14). Jesus never forced himself on anyone, and neither will I. But when the challenge is accepted—when hypocrites choose to suspend disbelief for even a brief moment—the Spirit of the Lord never fails to work profound miracles. The Lord delights in a repentant heart, and he loves to show off to skeptics who pause to say, *Lord, I believe! Help my unbelief!* (Mark 9:24). In these moments we experience blind eyes seeing again, deaf ears hearing, and hard hearts softening like butter in the warm glory glow of honor received.

In many minds, the line between conviction and condemnation is barely visible. When you don't get challenged much, any challenge can feel like condemnation. But we must remain open to the Spirit's loving correction. Only by receiving his rebuke can we humble ourselves and position our hearts to receive *any* honor, let alone double honor.

Reading the Room

If you want to reclaim the lost art of honor, you'll need to learn to read the room. If you're going to sit and eat before a king or queen, it's better to put a knife to your throat than to be a glutton (Proverbs 23:1–8). That said, you need to first be able to discern in the Spirit the kings and queens who are hiding right before you in plain sight. In time, you will learn to recognize those people worthy of honor in your midst—the often-overlooked nobodies and the spiritual giants alike. When you sense the power of the mantles they carry, you'll give them double the honor—not because they deserve it in their own strength, but because God chose them to wear the garment. Here are a few ways to find these precious ones.

Pay attention to people, not just to what they're saying. When you enter a room, do a quick scan with the Holy Spirit of who is present. Study facial expressions, posture and positioning, and body language. Are people engaged and ready? Are they distant or defensive? Are they smiling, scowling, or smirking? Are they standing or sitting? Open or guarded? Stay socially and supernaturally aware of what's really going on and follow the Spirit's prompts to invite people deeper into the conversation.

As a general rule, listen more than you speak. When you're speaking, you can't listen, so even if you're visiting as a celebrated keynote with wisdom to share, stay hungry and leave space in the room for others to shine. Pause frequently to check in with people, demonstrating that you care what they're thinking. Ask open, inviting questions to allow people to participate in the conversation without feeling pushy. Honoring prompts like "What are your thoughts?" and "Tell me more about that…" and "Given your experience, I'd love your take on this!" make people feel seen, heard, and loved.

Consider what you might not immediately see. When people fade into the background, it's often because we're not considering their current reality. What's happening in their life? What struggles are they facing? What unique dreams and anointings are they carrying, wondering if they're really worthy of honor in the first place? Ask for the Spirit's help to highlight to you people, places, things, and social dynamics that might indicate an opportunity to bestow honor. Resist the urge to disqualify people from honor because they're going through something you don't yet understand.

> ***Resist the urge to disqualify people from honor because they're going through something you don't yet understand.***

When you discover the grace and anointing in these hidden ones, bestow honor regardless of title or stature. You might catch their anointing and multiply it, or you might simply benefit from being in the presence of such a vitally important member of the body of Christ. Whatever the outcome, rest assured that honor begets honor. When we bestow it faithfully, it will double and triple and even quadruple in Jesus' name. The vast, limitless potential that comes with honor runs toe-to-toe with the Father's deep love for us. Grains of sand in the ocean don't even begin to cover the count: "How precious also are Your thoughts to me, O God! How great is the sum of them! If I should count them, they would be more in number than the sand; when I awake, I am still with You" (Psalm 139:17–18).

Giving Double Honor

Honor isn't something that's earned; it's bestowed. And although we are meant to give honor to all people, Scripture is clear that we are to give double honor to our elders—the ones who lead effectively and work hard at teaching and preaching (1 Timothy 5:17). This isn't some blanket statement that implies, *Honor your senior pastor and sit quietly and obediently underneath his or her unquestioned authority*. Far from it. This Scripture is about elders ruling *well*—not because of achieved title, wealth, power, influence, or even church growth numbers, but because they are steadfast guiding lights who are living godly, honorable lives worthy of emulating.

Once, a prominent Native American father of the faith presented me with a prayer shawl he had taken on a pilgrimage through all fifty US states in a spirit of reformation. This quite literal passing of his mantle to me overwhelmed me, and at first, I could not receive it. It was too precious. This anointed man, this well-ruling elder, was far more deserving of such a precious and sacred mantle than I. We went back and forth for what must've been an awkward while for onlookers, both of us ending up face down on the carpet before one another in a collective puddle of tears. And finally, it hit me: Refusing this mantle was refusing this most honorable elder's honor being bestowed on me! God wanted it passed down, so how could I refuse it? I carry that mantle of reformation with me to this day, honoring God by honoring his faithful servant.

Since then, I've been much more open to receiving honor bestowed, because I know the very act of receiving is also honor bestowed. When a Muslim family of strangers in India invited me and my ministry team to a traditional *mutton biryani* meal in their modest, dirt-floor home, I was eager to give them my yes—and I've been thankful that I did ever since. In Indian culture, guests eat first, then the men, then the women and children. As we feasted on a gourmet meal that probably cost a month of wages for this precious family, I was reminded of Mary Magdalene's sacrifice to her Savior at her sister Martha's home in John 12. She not only washed Jesus' feet with her hair and tears; she anointed them with perfume that likely cost more than a year's wages. She didn't hesitate. She didn't check her budget. She didn't even consider her cultural place as a Jewish woman, which, in Martha's opinion, should have been in the kitchen! She gave her all in unbridled honor. Although he surely knew what it cost the family, Jesus didn't refuse her. The onlookers were shocked and offended, but Jesus honored her and her sacrifice. He received her unusual (and some might have argued "unclean") gifts of perfume, tears, and time, and he made an example of her devotion that would last throughout the ages. Flash forward to that dirt-floor Indian kitchen filled with generous and hungry hosts. The family honored me—and I gave double honor back to them.

Submit, Serve, and Sow

The process for double honor is as simple as one, two, three—*submit*, *serve*, and *sow*. Granted, this level of honor isn't for everyone; it's for those kings and queens who are worthy of double honor. The Mary Magdalenes. The Billy Grahams. The Heidi Bakers. The Mother Theresas. The Benny Hinns. The Bill Johnsons. The mother who faithfully brings baked goods for Friday night recovery meetings. The elder who stays after service to sweep the foyer. Kings and queens of the faith who are ruling and reigning well.

Submit. Double honor requires an act of submission, one that honors individuals for who they are and what they carry, regardless of title, fame, or stature. This submission cannot be reluctant or manipulative, nor can it be by force or coercion. Submission dignifies the individual, honors the anointing on his or her life, and puts you in proximity to be blessed by that anointing.

Serve. Double honor requires at least some level of reciprocity. When someone is ruling and reigning well, chances are you or the ones you love and lead are benefiting from the unique anointing that person carries. If you want to show double honor, you must respond to this benefit. Provide a meal for a family in crisis. Stay late to help stack chairs or wipe tables. Send a handwritten note of gratitude and honor for a job well done. Even the simple act of asking how you can be of service can bridge relational gaps in community and multiply the anointing within your ranks.

Sow. Double honor requires you to bless and/or give back to those who rule and reign well. Giving toward the people and causes that move you with compassion is biblical. This concept is simple, but following through on it isn't easy. Now, sowing doesn't always require you to pull out your checkbook. (Although it very well might, so be ready.) It may require you to sow into someone's life through mentoring, discipleship, or even friendship. It might mean offering a listening ear, giving ideas and advice, or simply being available when someone needs you. God loves a joyful giver—and those worthy of double honor will almost always be worthy of your time, talent, and treasure.

For whatever reason, the strangers we met in India saw the anointing on my life and treated me as one worthy of double honor. Even in a predominantly Muslim culture, they invited me into their home and sat underneath my teaching (submitting). They cooked for me and treated me as a king (serving). They filled my belly and my soul with a sacrificially lavish meal (sowing). In receiving such honor, I was filled to overflowing and moved to share my portion with them. I submitted and ate my fill first, as was the custom, despite my gut instinct to insist that the family eat along with me (submitting). After I ate, I helped serve and honor our gracious hosts by filling their plates with food (serving). Then I shared mission field stories, giving them the greatest gift of all: the gospel (sowing).

Keep in mind, you can carry an office or title and not be anointed for it. Conversely, you can be anointed with no formal office or title. The complexities of the honor environment can leave you a little unsure, but here are some helpful ways to ensure you're honoring your elders well: If someone carries an earthly title with no discernible spiritual anointing for that title? Give them honor anyway. If someone carries an anointing with no title? Give them honor. If someone carries both a title and the anointing for that title? Give them *double* honor.

True promotion comes from God, not from man. And when you learn to read the room, you'll learn to honor all and give double honor where double honor is due.

Submit. Serve. Sow. Yes, even when you don't feel like it. Yes, even when you feel disregarded. And yes, even when you don't receive that double portion of honor back from those you lift up. Go low anyway. God sees you, he hears you, he loves you, and he will bring you reciprocal honor in his kingdom realm when you serve him faithfully. Double honor is readily available to everyone, but only the worthy can receive it. So read the room. Stay unoffendable. And always remember that to be worthy of double honor, you'd better be willing to give it. Are you willing?

Honorable Reflections

What makes someone worthy of double honor?

What might bestowing double honor look like?

Which is most challenging for you: submitting, serving, or sowing? Why?

Is there anybody in your life who you feel is worthy of double honor? Why?

9

Dispelling Dishonor

Let nothing be done through selfish ambition or conceit, but in lowliness of mind let each esteem others better than himself. Let each of you look out not only for his own interests, but also for the interests of others.

Philippians 2:3–4 NKJV

Where there is disrespect and dishonor, normally grace and mercy disappear meanwhile privileges and favors tend to automatically cease.

Dr. Lucas D. Shallua

By now, you've come to understand that dishonor, at its core, is a sin. But dishonor is more than just a sin—it's a curse. Dishonor breeds division, opening wide the door for Leviathan (envy), Jezebel (seduction), and other "spiritual hosts of wickedness in the heavenly places" (Ephesians 6:12 NKJV) to infiltrate. I firmly believe the vast cultural and generational gaps in society and in the church exist in part because we have tolerated dishonor for far too long. Dishonor is the opposite of honor, the currency of heaven, and those who deal in dishonor will have no power, authority, or access to resources in God's kingdom. Those who weaponize dishonor through jealousy, envy, manipulation, coercion, gaslighting, slander, and accusation perform witchcraft under dishonor's generational curse.

Oftentimes the curse of dishonor will take shape as a spirit of narcissism. I've seen it a hundred times. It starts with a sob story that gets overshared, embellished, and then blown out of proportion—a strategy of the enemy to divide the brethren. Shared offense festers, false narratives become our truth, and people turn against one another and against organizations. Jesus' Matthew 18 style of church discipline goes out the window, and distance and separation reign. This rebellious, narcissistic spirit often stems from a root of rejection or abandonment—a perceived lack of love, covering, and authentic relationship. Whether the sob story is true or not, dishonor breeds like bacteria and festers in these proverbial wounds.

Dishonor rarely kicks off in grand dramatic fashion. It builds subtly and over time. Dishonor can start with an eye roll or an attitude. A single slanderous word or prideful questioning of authority can spark wild flames of hatred in the body of Christ. While we all have the freedom to ask questions in good faith, a competitive spirit of oppositional defiance can turn curiosity to callousness in a heartbeat. When those worthy of honor by title, office, or anointing are bullied by inexperienced, uncredentialed, and entitled brats who think they know better and are better, the collective opportunity for double honor is jeopardized. Mantles are torches that must be passed. They cannot be snatched from an elder for personal gain. Neither can they be replaced with a counterfeit anointing.

Friend, if we are going to reclaim the lost art of honor in our generation, we are going to need to do more than just show, bestow, and walk in honor. We must also be willing to dispel dishonor whenever and wherever we encounter it, coming against these spirits of wickedness in Jesus' name.

You see, there should be no competition in the body of Christ. Zero. Zilch. Nada! We are *one*—and when one of us ascends to higher levels, it benefits us all. The arm should not wage war on the leg, and the hand should not wage war on the eye. We cannot continue to war against one another and ourselves. As one body, we share in the successes and failures, joy and pain, gain and loss. The only competitor you have is the devil—Satan himself. Our defeated foe rages in his loss, doing everything he can to trick us into believing the lie that he still has power over sin and death. The more we come into agreement with the truth about our oneness in Christ, the more we can let go of the enemy's vain, divisive, unoriginal arguments—arguments that will one day dissolve completely. And above all, "Keep your heart with all diligence, for out of it spring the issues of life" (Proverbs 4:23 NKJV).

Character Assassination

Dishonor can happen anywhere and at any time, in ways you may never have expected. Earnest church-parlor prayer meetings turn into gossip sessions. Safe-haven sanctuaries become torture chambers of discrimination, marginalization, and abuse. Pre-service green rooms create green space where predatory species exploit and expose. In every corner of the kingdom, apostles and prophets are being looked down upon and dishonored by other men and women of God. Doors are closed, and disassociations commence. Wannabe influencers tear down the anointed ones in a spirit of harassment and character assassination. I've seen it. I've experienced it firsthand.

Why is dishonoring behavior so rampant in society and in the church? It's simple: People *love* drama. They gravitate to it like a moth to a flame. When people have boring lives, they love to insert themselves into the middle of everyone else's messes, pointing out perceived faults and failures so they can feel better about their own. The dopamine rush of superiority dominates relational discourse, and we become willing to "unfriend" or "block" people—not just on social media but in real life.

Several years ago, I was scheduled to minister at Yonggi Cho's prayer mountain in Seoul, South Korea, the largest church congregation in the world. I was beyond excited, but not for the reasons you might think. Numbers are impressive, and international travel is enticing. But most significantly, as a Korean American, I have a divine birthright to be in my mother country and to minister to God's people there.

When I arrived in Seoul, my momentum came to a screeching halt when the pastors received a letter of complaint about me and my ministry the day before I was supposed to preach. Not only did the prayer mountain congregant who wrote the letter dislike my bleached-blond hair, my Gucci sunglasses, and my American bravado; apparently, the letter had words like *false prophet* and *blasphemy* to describe my ministry activities. Because showing honor to a congregant is essential in their culture, the pastors rescinded my invitation to speak.

Admittedly, I was shocked. Instead of reacting in frustration, however, I immediately went to the Lord in prayer. He had brought me this far—halfway across the world—and I knew it couldn't have been for nothing. So I did the only thing I could do. I surrendered the situation to the Lord and asked him to redeem it. I asked him to honor me as I did my sincere best to honor Yonggi Cho's house.

Some might have been on the next flight home, but I chose to stay, learn, grow, and be humbled.

Early the next morning, I found out that after deep prayer and collective discernment, the pastors had changed their minds. They wanted to honor me, my journey, and the gifts God had anointed me to share. They asked me to minister to a relatively small group of five hundred people in a Friday night service, where more than fifty people experienced some form of miraculous healing. Hearts were softened. Souls were saved. Bodies were healed in Jesus' name. One unforgettably precious person was healed of a debilitating disease that night. This person sprang up from a wheelchair and sprinted through the auditorium praising God. Unbeknownst to me, a video of the healing was posted to social media and went viral. Seemingly overnight, I became a brand-new installation in the "Who's Who of the Charismatic Zoo."

I don't share this story of honor to gloat or self-promote. I share it because the outcome of this preciously intimate time of ministry was even greater than the miracles of that night. Everyone in the family of the person who was healed was saved during that Friday night service—including the family member who had written the disparaging letter about me. A week later, God's mercy led the letter writer to send a new letter of apology to the pastors. This once-wary congregant had witnessed God's healing through my time of ministry and had gotten to know the real me—not a false persona of me—and then chose to honor me and the anointing I carried. In this wild, unexpected place of grace, the power of God on display turned dishonor into double honor. The next time I went to Seoul, I was invited to minister to the crowd in a sanctuary that seats seven thousand people.

One might expect to receive a lower measure of honor from the world's largest megachurch. After all, who am I to teach, preach at, or minister to Yonggi Cho's massive flock? They didn't know me from Adam—beyond what they saw on the internet, anyway. But when they saw me, they all got to know the real me: an image-bearer of the living God (nothing more, nothing less), equipped and empowered to bring the kingdom wherever I go. When I moved in honor amid disappointment across the world in Seoul, honor came back to me threefold.

The Home Front

Considering this round-the-world example, logic might tell you that the people who know you—like *really* know you—would naturally try to honor you in all you do. And yet, most prophets find honor the hardest to come by in their hometowns. As Jesus said, "A prophet is not without honor except in his own country, among his own relatives, and in his own house" (Mark 6:4 NKJV).

I have often found these words of Jesus true even in my own history. For example, in pastoring my beloved SoCal church, Open Heavens World, many people have come and gone. It is painful to see the lack of honor at times because they can see me as a "common young pastor" rather than as a global voice and worldwide evangelist. The honor I receive while traveling sometimes seems more overwhelming and generous than what I receive from my local church family. Despite our apostolic community's shared passion for worship, fellowship, teachings, and missional efforts in Los Angeles and around the world, there are times when overfamiliarity can fester. Instead of "Dr. Ben Lim, prophet to the nations," I'm just seen as "Ben." And although being fully seen and fully known by my people of peace is pure joy, there have been some instances (not many or frequent!) in which I haven't always been fully loved or fully understood by the ones who by right *should* know me best.

Southern California is a tough crowd. Locals are usually either intimidated by, offended by, or generally uninterested in me. At regional events, I'm invited to attend but rarely to minister. I'm seen as a young local pastor with little to offer the ones who know me all too well. Sadly, this is across-the-board true. It was true for our forefathers, and it will likely be true for you one day too. This overfamiliarity may call you out from the comforts of your hometown so you can do what Jesus did: go where you're celebrated, not where you're tolerated.

I take great comfort in knowing that Jesus "gets me" on this issue. The people who watched him grow up in Nazareth refused to honor the office that he carried as a rabbi and prophet, and they also refused to honor his anointing as Messiah. How could they? For thirty years, they had known Jesus as a relatively unremarkable Jewish guy, working, worshiping, and living life like everyone else. And then, *boom!* Jesus steps into his messianic role, leaving the ones who knew him best thinking, *Umm…him?* People weren't able to embrace the powerful mindset shift it would take to adjust to this "new" Jesus.

The wild part is that even his own mother and brothers struggled to fully trust, support, and honor Jesus at first (3:21). So why would we expect any different from our people, the ones who know us best? In your own life shifts and seasons, have people struggled to adjust to the "new creation" you've become as one who has been elevated, metamorphosed, and even transfigured? If so, you and Jesus have a lot in common.

Change in your life creates confusion and chaos in the lives of those who were perhaps more comfortable with the old you. When you've grown in wisdom and you no longer relate to your culture of origin, you may one day find yourself speaking a different language than your elders and peers—literally and figuratively. Try as they might to love and honor the gold in you, they simply can't relate to the revelation you've experienced. Jesus' own life shifted dramatically when he stepped into his calling, and it was hard for people in his home country to receive it. So he didn't do many miracles there. Yes, he did some, but not as many as he would have if the people had positioned themselves in humility to receive.

An Ichabod Spirit

The condition of the heart will determine the amount of blessings God chooses to pour out on his people. It's less about belief and more about openness and spiritual curiosity, both individually and corporately. Cities and even nations can reject Christ, embodying an Ichabod spirit that grieves the Holy Spirit over the glory departed.

This often-forgotten character, Ichabod, was an actual man in Scripture whose family was living under the priestly authority of the prophet Samuel. On the day Ichabod was born, his world fell apart in one sudden swoop. His mother, unnamed in Scripture, dies in childbirth. His evil father, Phinehas, dies in battle. His high-priest grandfather, Eli, falls off his seat to his death, snapping his neck. And to top it all off? The Philistines steal the ark of the covenant from the Israelites, leading the Israelites to believe that the glory of God had departed from Israel (1 Samuel 4:21). The result? Invasion. Destruction. Captivity. Generational slavery.

In her dying breath, Ichabod's mother gave her baby son a name that translates to "without honor" because of the devastation surrounding his birth. And unfortunately, far too many of us carry

Ichabod's less-than-honorable namesake to this day—a generational curse that's tearing the church and the world apart.

The wild part about Ichabod is that we don't really know what happened to him next. He didn't have a good family name, so nobody would have expected anything good to come from him. We don't know what Ichabod's childhood as an orphan was like, nor do we know if he was ever able to redeem his family legacy by becoming a priest himself. But we do know that Ichabod didn't let the dishonor of his family of origin determine his future or the future of his people. God didn't depart from the Israelites forever: the Philistines returned the ark of the covenant, complete with a guilt offering (1 Samuel 6). In time, Ichabod's nephew Ahijah became a priest, showcasing the cultural and familial redemption that can happen when we refuse to let our circumstances define us (14:3).

When the glory departs, the elders die. Literally and figuratively. The glory is who we are, the very presence of Jehovah in us that is worthy of honor. Where there is dishonor, prophets are pushed away and the door swings wide open for invasion, attack, and all-out warfare.

Take Jinja, Uganda, for example, a lake city at the base of the Nile River that was once referred to as the "Switzerland" of Africa. In 1990, a Christ for all Nations (CfaN) crusade with the prophet Reinhard Bonnke was violently stopped by military order of the governor, some say over some equipment stolen from CfaN's tech team. Bonnke shook the dust off, literally and figuratively, and moved on. In mere months, droughts ensued, the country went broke, and the governor went insane and was removed from office. Jinja opened the door to attack by rejecting God's prophet, and the city was cursed for thirty years because of it.[25]

Perhaps you too have been put into a box. Misunderstood, despised, rejected of men (Isaiah 53). Perhaps, like Ichabod, no one ever expected anything from you, and people will have a hard time accepting anything from you. Perhaps you too have been overlooked because of familiarity. Perhaps you too feel despised and rejected of men. As you walk in honor no matter what, go where you're celebrated, not where you're tolerated. When you do? You too will be given the grace to do even greater miracles than Jesus did, by the power of the Holy Spirit (John 14:12).

How to Dispel Dishonor

Honor begets honor, and dishonor begets dishonor with devastating consequences. When a man or woman of God is dishonored, the grace that person carries on his or her life doesn't operate as it could—or, perhaps, *should*. This will all too often result in the prophet leaving town, dusting off his or her sandals and heading for a new land where he or she will be celebrated rather than just tolerated. Now, one way or the other, the prophet will receive the honor due. God will see to it. But when a prophet is dishonored, cities and even nations can miss out on participating in the coming kingdom of God as prophesied through his servants.

When you make a conscious choice to walk in honor, the Lord will heighten your senses to discern dishonor in the natural and supernatural world. An elder passing judgment on the newfangled ideas of an emerging leader. Maturing youth refusing to acknowledge the foundation their forefathers sacrificed for so they could build. Condescending glances. Toxic words. Manipulative, narcissistic, familiarity-minded spirits. You will come to recognize them all. Whether dishonor is playing out right before your eyes or you become newly convicted of your own less-than-honorable dealings, you will be moved with compassion and anointed with the oil of justice to come against that spirit of dishonor in Jesus' name.

Easier said than done, I know. But your ability and willingness to dispel dishonor will help resurrect and reclaim honor in the church, in society, and around the world.

In my experience, dispelling dishonor is best accomplished in one of three ways:

- *Say* something.
- *Pray* something.
- *Do* something.

When dishonor surfaces and you sense the Spirit's nudge, *be ready to say something*. Let the Holy Spirit speak words of invitation or challenge in humility and grace. Ask questions. Offer perspective. Be willing to name the elephant in the room and speak words of reconciliation in the face of dishonor. Whether you address the situation promptly by reading the room and responding in love or you request private sidebars for these critical conversations, if you see something, say something.

When dishonor surfaces and you're feeling unwilling or unable to speak up, *be ready to pray something*. Share the perceived dishonor with the Lord and ask him how he feels about it. Ask him to open your mind, soften your heart, and empower your spirit to know what he wants you to say or do—if anything. Speak with authority over dishonor and send it straight to hell. Welcome grace, peace, and love, and ask for a fresh revelation of honor in the situation. Some see prayer as a cop-out, but let me be straight with you: If you're not willing to pray something, you'd better think twice before saying or doing anything to dispel dishonor. It will probably be out of your prideful flesh.

When dishonor surfaces and your heart for justice kicks in, *be ready to do something*. While speaking and praying are definitely on the to-do list, consider creative ways that you might come against a spirit of dishonor with an opposite spirit of honor. Look for ways to serve weary, unappreciated prophets with your time, talent, treasure, and influence. Acknowledge the God-given potential in an emerging (or stumbling) leader and invite him or her into growth. Honor forgotten elders' perspectives and contributions. Go out of your way to celebrate them before men. Whatever the spirit of dishonor presents, respond in the opposite spirit and do something.

Honor and dishonor cannot coexist.
One is holy; one is not.
One is of the Lord; one is of the enemy.

Honor and dishonor cannot coexist. One is holy; one is not. One is of the Lord; one is of the enemy. Dispelling dishonor simply involves a willingness to name dishonor when you see it and to dispel it however the Lord asks you to. It's risky sometimes, I'm aware, but God will protect you. In fact, the Word says that when God is pleased with you, he will even win your enemies over in your favor: "When a man's ways please the Lord, He makes even his enemies to be at peace with him" (Proverbs 16:7).

Do you believe it? Are you willing to engage in courageous conversations, bold prayers, and brave actions to dispel dishonor in your family, your church, or your community? When you do, God will bless you—and he may even call you to be an ambassador of honor to the nations.

Rejection or Protection?

Emerging leaders whom I disciple will often ask me how I'm invited to preach so much. I rarely know what to say, other than that I do my best to have a good name, build and maintain relationships, and unapologetically carry out my unique anointing. I honor myself and others, and others honor me. That said, I know full well that I have a pretty specific kingdom niche, which means people in mainstream Christianity don't always acknowledge or reciprocate what I have to offer. I'm not entirely sure they're supposed to.

The reality is, people won't always see the grace on your life when you walk in honor. This shouldn't come as a surprise to you, and it should not offend you. People can't honor who you are in the Lord when they don't understand who you are in him. They may know of you, but they don't yet know what they're honoring in you! And while it's rarely (if ever) your responsibility to make them understand what you carry, it *is* your responsibility to give them grace and space as they suspend disbelief to try to better understand.

There's a time and season for everything. Worthy of honor as you are, there are times and even seasons when God keeps you hidden in his wings. It's important for you to understand that this is not rejection. It's protection. What you carry is precious enough to protect from those who might seek to show you false honor with a hidden agenda. I'm going to give it to you straight: The *last* thing you need as an emerging leader in the body of Christ is the dishonor of flattery. It will poison you to the things of God and leave you clinging desperately to the opinions of man.

Dishonor is demonic. It's distracting, draining, and destructive. It not only pushes God away; it also pushes his mantles away, keeping you from fulfilling your life's calling. This is why the Holy

Spirit can be not only grieved (Ephesians 4:30) but quenched: "Do not quench the Spirit. Do not despise prophecies. Test all things; hold fast to what is good. Abstain from every form of evil" (1 Thessalonians 5:19–22). In Paul's letter to the church in Thessalonica, he insists that the Holy Spirit can be both pleased and displeased. The Spirit is extraordinarily sensitive. Sin keeps God at arm's length, and dishonor perpetuates the cycle.

Now, it's important for us to remember that God doesn't distance himself from you or me because of dishonor. He is a covenantal God. You are one with your Creator in Christ by the power of the Spirit. And to him, you are holy and blameless because of what Christ did. When sin enters the equation, God doesn't put you at arm's length. It's the other way around. When your sinful behavior can no longer coexist with a holy God, you distance yourself—often without knowing it—embracing a false theology that breeds dishonor. Do you struggle to maintain healthy relationships? Are you quick to leave when people or organizations don't check all your boxes? Do you feel entitled to a critical spirit because you know you're right? If so, you're most likely dealing with a deep root of dishonor that must be dispelled.

Dispel Dishonor with Honor

Honor is a grace that attracts more of what it has already obtained. Read that again: *Honor is a grace that attracts more of what it has already obtained.*

You see, you can't receive *more* of what you don't yet have. You can only receive more of what you already possess in some measure. Honor begets honor, which means honor is the source of honor—originating from Honor himself. Even if you've been walking in or through a spirit of dishonor, in Christ you do have honor in your possession—a powerful tool in your kingdom tool belt. The sooner you realize this, the sooner you'll be able and willing to dispel dishonor with honor.

Honor begets honor, which means honor is the source of honor—originating from Honor himself.

You don't have to strive to get God to come close. He's already with you, already for you. More than that, his Spirit is living in you. You bear his divine image whether you realize it or not, because it's how he created you. And because of Jesus Christ, you've been reconciled with a holy God who sees you as perfect, holy, and blameless. You and God? You're already unified. That said, you can absolutely attract more of God by putting a lifestyle of honor on display. Honor attracts God as the budding flower's sweet nectar attracts the honeybee. What's more, when you walk in honor, you shine so brightly that you stand out—drawing more of God's presence to put on display for a dark, desolate, and increasingly desperate world.

God is drawn to honor, purity, righteousness, obedience, and humility, but he opposes pride (Psalm 138:6). Dishonor, impurity, unrighteousness, disobedience, and pride actually push God away, creating a perception of distance and separation from God that enables sin. Dishonor promotes spiritual isolation, and it must be stopped.

Today, young people often think they know what's best. When it comes to philosophical, environmental, cultural, and social crises of the day, they claim they know best by screaming it from the digital mountaintops. But true vessels of honor don't scream. And it's because a true vessel of honor is not merely heard but *felt*—the heavy *kāḇôḏ* glory that vessel carries is tangible.

I occasionally joke that the loudest barking dogs in ministry are the chihuahuas of the kingdom. If you're a little dog person, my apologies for this potentially divisive analogy. (At least I didn't make it about cats.) But I'd much rather be quiet and still in my authority and position before the Lord than be tooting my own horn about how powerful, anointed, and mighty I am! This is because true authority is self-controlled, meek, and humble—not self-proclaiming, self-announced, and self-appointed. To me, having a quiet strength is a much better demonstration of being an authority figure than is acting like a whiny, yippy, powerless little pooch who can fit in your mom's purse. Ankle biters are not anointed. Just sayin'.

The dishonor of youth cuts off the wisdom, inheritance, and blessing that are meant to be passed down through the generations. The same can be said for the dishonor of elders who are unwilling or unable to pass the mantle. Anointings from God will certainly look different generation to generation because each and every one of us is, in his or her own way, born "for such a time as this" (Esther 4:14). But honor must originate from honor, not from rebellion or fascism. Rebellion is attractive to the prideful spirit, presenting itself falsely as a viable reaction to injustice and even perceived dishonor. Fascism is attractive to would-be fathers and mothers who'd rather keep the glory for themselves than raise up a generation. None of us are innocent of or immune to dishonor's curse, which is why we must be vigilant—ready to fight dishonor with honor in Jesus' name.

When you fight dishonor with more dishonor, you engage in demonic division and witchcraft. Sin begets sin. Hate begets hate. Wrath begets wrath. And those who won't acknowledge this truth will fall *hard* from grace. Dishonor destroys relationships, closes doors, and lays down necessary defenses designed to protect the brethren. Dishonor metastasizes by overinflating the individual and corporate ego to destroy everything in its path, salting the earth behind it. When this happens, we'll not only be unable to receive the Lord's prophets; we'll also be unable to enjoy the fruit of the Word they despairingly sow into the rubble and ruin.

When we fight dishonor with honor, we foster a culture where people not only feel welcome; they also don't want to leave. Time flies in a spirit of honor. Gold, pearls, and precious stones are released in the supernatural world. Guests long for your community and count the days to a time when they can come back to stay in a place where they can be the truest and best version of themselves. This is the difference between a *visitation* and a *habitation* of God. When people have a visitation, they leave and often never come back. When people have a habitation, they're home.

Consider your own community cultures. Do people want to come and stay? Does *God* want to come and stay? Like Obed-Edom, are you willing to drop everything to host the very presence of God (in the ark of the covenant) for three months so it might bless your house? If so, you are a true habitation of the Lord, and God will provide safe-haven sanctuary to many in and through you. You'll be a hub of glory for the kingdom.

This principle applies in all areas of life: spiritually, personally, and even professionally. When you honor God, he will honor you before men (1 Samuel 2:30; John 12:26). People mistakenly think they can climb a corporate ladder of success on the backs of their peers and subordinates. They'll do just about anything to get to the next level. This is dishonor. An act of the flesh that results in promotion will require additional acts of the flesh to maintain it. Will you compromise? How far is too far? How much is too much? If slow obedience is disobedience, let's go ahead and call fleshly ambition what it is: demonic. Those who engage in works of the flesh for self-promotion will not inherit the kingdom of God (Galatians 5:19–21).

Let nothing be done out of dishonor or pride. Instead, have the mind of Christ. He went low, humbling himself before God our Father, who then exalted him:

> Therefore if there is any consolation in Christ, if any comfort of love, if any fellowship of the Spirit, if any affection and mercy, fulfill my joy by being like-minded, having the same love, being of one accord, of one mind. *Let nothing be done through selfish ambition or conceit*, but in lowliness of mind let each esteem others better than himself. Let each of you look out not only for his own interests, but also for the interests of others.
>
> *Let this mind be in you which was also in Christ Jesus*, who, being in the form of God, did not consider it robbery to be equal with God, but made Himself of no reputation, taking the form of a bondservant, and coming in the likeness of men. And being found in appearance as a man, *He humbled Himself and became obedient to the point of death, even the death of the cross.* Therefore God also has highly exalted Him and given Him the

> name which is above every name, that at the name of Jesus every knee should bow, of those in heaven, and of those on earth, and of those under the earth, and that every tongue should confess that Jesus Christ is Lord, to the glory of God the Father. (Philippians 2:1–11, emphasis added)

You breed what you carry. You breed what you allow. And what you tolerate will become your future. It's my prayer that you will choose to fight to dispel dishonor so the church of Jesus Christ can be a welcoming, inviting habitation for the Holy Spirit and a welcoming host for a move of God.

Honorable Reflections

Have people ever treated you with overfamiliarity? What was the result?

Have you ever treated someone with overfamiliarity? How can you keep from doing this?

What happens when you feel dishonored?

What happens when a prophet is dishonored in a community or region?

10

Honor: A Prophet's Reward

"He who receives you receives Me, and he who receives Me receives Him who sent Me."

MATTHEW 10:40 NKJV

Honour may not win power, but it wins respect. And respect earns power.

ISHIDA MITSUNARI, JAPANESE WARRIOR

As a minister of the gospel, I believe that God calls prophets to speak his word and represent him to the people. In return for their obedience, God promises to reward them. What's more, God promises to pass along that same reward to those who choose to honor the prophets through hospitality, generosity, and other types of support. Their blessing can quite literally be passed on to you as a mantle. That is, if you are ready to receive it.

By now, you've sensed my urgency in preparing you to be on the receiving end of honor—not by puffing yourself up but by going low. Bestowing honor in authentic community—honoring prophets, elders, and anyone you encounter who carries the divine DNA of God—is the very essence of walking in honor. If you want to be part of reclaiming the lost art of honor, you need to be able and willing to receive prophets so you can carry on their reward.

Scripture is clear in Matthew 10:41 that "he who receives a prophet in the name of a prophet shall receive a prophet's reward" (NKJV). The very next sentence in that same verse says something similar, but distinctive: "And he who receives a righteous man in the name of a righteous man shall receive a righteous man's reward." This classifies two kinds of people you can receive reward through: the prophets and the righteous ones. But in order to receive this "prophet's reward," you will need to honor them. Beyond lodging, meals, per diem, and words spoken, you will need to go low—and in some cases lay down your life—to honor the anointing they carry. The Lord rewards those who bestow honor and love with pure, genuine hearts.

The Lord rewards those who bestow honor and love with pure, genuine hearts.

What is the prophet's reward anyway? Why would someone want or need or seek out such a thing? Contrary to popular belief, the prophet's reward is not always financial—or even *material*, for that matter. The prophet's reward is spiritual, something eternal. The prophets of God are promised a special closeness to him that provides a deeper understanding of his perfect ways. Prophets are given deeper insight into the mysteries of the kingdom, which strategically enables them to discern the plans and purposes of God. Equipped with revelation, God uses prophets to bring about powerful manifestations of his presence and power. Miracles, signs, and wonders often accompany their ministries as they speak forth the word of the Lord with boldness and authority. And when you receive a prophet? You will receive as a reward a measure of the mantle that he or she carries. Anyone who receives a prophet will receive the same reward as that prophet. Similarly, anyone who receives a righteous person will receive the same reward as that righteous person.

Now, God doesn't reward people for no reason. The prophet's reward is a bonus—extra reserves of favor and grace that come upon you naturally and supernaturally, whether you realize it or not. Some rewards manifest in your life on earth today, while others are stored up in heaven for eternity. These rewards go far beyond the gift of salvation, which is free and for everyone. We're talking next-level, extra tools that will not only ease your time on earth but will build a stronger and more fulfilling kingdom life in you now and into eternity.

While there is no competition in the kingdom—at least not in the sense that honor must be taken from one person in order to be bestowed upon another—some of us will experience a spiritual "leveling up" that others never do because of our willingness to go deeper and reach higher in our good works. It's similar to being on an Olympic relay team. You celebrate the wins of every team member: broken records; first, second, and third place finishes; and, of course, any medal that brings honor to your country. But those same runners are also in it for a personal record, knowing that their PR is not only a personal best but a win for the collective group. Being part of a team means working hard, but it also means trusting your teammates to work hard as well. Moreover, it means celebrating their successes as if they are your own, because they are! The same rings true in the kingdom of God. There is no competition, but there is absolutely a race to be run:

> Therefore we also, since we are surrounded by so great a cloud of witnesses, let us lay aside every weight, and the sin which so easily ensnares us, and let us run with endurance the race that is set before us, looking unto Jesus, the author and finisher of our faith, who for the joy that was set before Him endured the cross, despising the shame, and has sat down at the right hand of the throne of God. (Hebrews 12:1–2)

It's important to remember that there are never any "losers" in this race. But there will always be winners when it comes to honor. There is a healthy and friendly competition in the kingdom of God that focuses not on personal achievement but on elevating others. No matter how gifted you are, there will always be someone better and higher—more anointed, more prophetic, even more sold-out for the Lord than you are. Honoring this reality positions you to receive from these precious prophets and benefit from a prophet's reward. We must always be pushing for our personal best in this friendly competition, continually outdoing one another in honor (Romans 12:10). And we must collectively hold one another accountable to the same, bringing our best to our kingdom work as part of our shared expectations within a culture of honor.

Friend, we need one another to work hard, and we need each other to win! We can't skate by standing on the shoulders of our elders. Nor can we finish our race by trampling over the ones we're called to love and lead. Works without faith are pretty pointless in the kingdom, but faith without works is dead (James 2:14–26). Let your desire to serve the Lord by receiving his prophets flow from a place of true faith, humble surrender, and authentic relationship. There is always more available to you in the Lord's upside-down kingdom—and it will require you to go low so that you can lift others. In this way, you will be all that God has called you to be.

It's true that even those who do the bare minimum are "in" by definition: "If you confess with your mouth the Lord Jesus and believe in your heart that God has raised Him from the dead, you will be saved" (Romans 10:9). But who wants to give the bare minimum to the One who paid it all? Friend, you and I were made for more than this! You are destined for greatness, not mediocrity! You bear the image of the living God! His promise to you is clear: When you go above and beyond, you will be rewarded above and beyond:

> "Rejoice in that day and leap for joy! For indeed your reward is great in heaven, for in like manner their fathers did to the prophets." (Luke 6:23 NKJV)
>
> "Rejoice and be exceedingly glad, for great is your reward in heaven, for so they persecuted the prophets who were before you." (Matthew 5:12 NKJV)
>
> "And behold, I am coming quickly, and My reward is with Me, to give to every one according to his work." (Revelation 22:12 NKJV)

A Lack of Sound Teaching

We don't teach on the prophet's reward much in the church, and I think I know why. Well-meaning teachers think we might exploit the prophet's reward concept for personal gain, and they think this is because so many of us have, in fact, confused honor with idolatry. To honor a prophet is an act of worship, but to worship a prophet is an act of witchcraft. And the level of pastor and prophet worship we see in today's church is downright scary. Honoring godly men and women does not, in fact, make them gods—and we would do well to remember it.

The temptation toward celebrity thinking in Christian circles is one of the most dangerous threats to the modern church of Jesus Christ. When prophets, teachers, preachers, evangelists, and apostles are idolized by the flock instead of honored, Christ ceases to be the center of our worship, and we open wide the door for corruption. The people willingly worship a man or woman over God, and that man or woman forgets himself or herself. Mantles turn to absolute power in that person's mind, and what was meant to be an anointing passed down for generations dries up. As a result, the gifts and mantles our leaders carry are commoditized—bought and sold in the temple right beside the money changers' tables.

While we must remain aware of people's respective anointings so we might honor them and receive from them, we must resist the urge to name-drop, shoulder-brush, and sweet-talk our way into places of greater favor with the Lord. God sees right through this demonic strategy, and He won't allow you to prosper in it for long. The ways in which we broken humans have wrongfully interpreted passages of Scripture on the prophet's reward teeter on the line of a false prosperity gospel—where your own health and wealth trump the Greatest Commandment and the Great Commission that goes along with it. Think about these questions:

- What good are rewards if you fail to "love the Lord your God with all your heart, with all your soul, and with all your mind" (Matthew 22:37)?

- What good are rewards if you fail to "love your neighbor as yourself" (v. 39)?
- What good are rewards if you and I fail to "go…and make disciples of all nations, baptizing them in the name of the Father and of the Son and of the Holy Spirit, teaching them to obey everything" that Jesus commanded (28:18–20)?
- What's honor all about if not simply standing in the presence of the Lord our God?

I believe God is mobilizing a generation of emerging leaders with sound teaching on this powerfully misunderstood yet critically important subject. And if you're reading this book, chances are you may be one of them. Are you willing to receive this prophetic invitation? Are you willing to receive a prophet's reward? Are you willing to reclaim honor and pass the mantle on to the next generation—and the next, and the next?

When you honor a prophet, you *will* receive the prophet's reward. It's a by-product of your faithfulness when it comes to reclaiming the lost art of honor. But the reward itself can't be the primary reason why you bestow honor. We honor because the Lord commands it. Period.

The Pathway of the Prophet's Reward

From a conceptual standpoint, the prophet's reward is much like hidden treasure—gold, rubies, diamonds, and pearls of great price reserved for the Lord's prophets and available to anyone willing to honor those prophets. While there is no literal treasure map to read or linear chart to course, there is a pathway to a prophet's reward. This pathway unfolds before you as you walk obediently in honor, keeping step with Christ.

In my own experience, God will rarely give you direction for more than a few steps forward at a time. Any more than this, and we'd begin to make our own way in our own strength. The Lord never promised to give us all the answers and all the clarity we seek, but he did say he would be with us to the very end of the age. As you walk in honor, you can trust that he will make your paths straight and narrow, leading you in the way everlasting. Honor the Lord, honor yourself, and honor the prophets, and you will see the pathway to a prophet's reward unfold before your very eyes. The prophet's reward is affirmation from your heavenly Father that you are doing honor right—that you are becoming more and more like the person of Jesus Christ every day.

You've probably rightfully assumed that this hidden treasure rarely takes shape as literal precious metals and jewels. It can be in that form, of course—look at our friends Solomon and Sheba's queen, for example. But being focused only on earthly treasures in this instance is sorely limiting. The prophet's reward is something far more valuable than any earthly treasures we could hope for or imagine—let alone enjoy!

The prophet's reward is called a "reward" because it comes with intense challenge. When you honor a prophet, you take on a portion of his or her anointing—and a portion of his or her spiritual warfare. The obstacles the prophet faces will become your obstacles—and most times, in greater measure than the prophet before you! I dare say this is why so few people receive a full-on double portion of the prophet's reward. They're too afraid to put their life on the line by associating with the prophet publicly, too soft to take on the discouragement that comes with the prophet's mantle, or too weak to carry the race's baton forward on their own.

This is heavy stuff, I'm aware. But it's important that you know what you're getting into with anointings. The heavier the glory, the heavier the warfare. The greater the mantle, the greater the persecution. If you really want a prophet's reward, it's going to cost you. Only when you pass the test of the anointing's warfare will you receive your reward.

The prophet's reward, in its truest essence, is deeper friendship with God. It's a legacy of generational blessing, the fruit of your labor and the labor of the ones who came before you. Even when our elders fail to give us what we need, we can trust that God will. The psalmist says, "The secret of the Lord is with those who fear Him, and He will show them His covenant" (Psalm 25:14). When you healthily fear, revere, love, and honor the Lord your God, he will share his secrets with you, his most beloved.

The prophet's reward is both community and covenant—being in relationship with God's children of all generations and seeing his legacy grow via our availability, willingness, and obedience. Your inheritance—and theirs—awaits you on the other side of honor.

What a Prophet's Reward Means

Let's look more closely at several specific things that a prophet's reward means for us: greater gifts, greater impartation, greater revelation, greater encounters, open doors, kingdom connections, and increased authority.

A prophet's reward means *greater gifts*. The Lord will enhance your giftings, electrifying your prayer life and allowing you to walk with authority in your anointing in this realm. You'll heal the sick, cleanse the lepers, raise the dead, and cast out demons in his name (Matthew

10:8). You'll do these and even greater things than Christ did when he walked the earth (John 14:12). It sounds crazy, but it's true!

A prophet's reward means *greater impartation*. You'll not only be able to receive more fully from the Lord; you'll also be able to give and receive more completely with other men and women of God. This transference is critically important to passing the mantle of anointing from generation to generation, and it's essential for our work of multiplying missional disciples on this earth as part of the Great Commission.

A prophet's reward means *greater revelation*. God will not only share with you his secrets (Psalm 25:14); he will also speak to you plainly in ways that best resonate with your spirit. He may reveal new contextual truth in Scripture passages you've read hundreds of times before. He may reveal things that are permissible but no longer edifying in your life, and he may strip you of your idols. He may invite you into seeing the divine DNA in the most unlikely vessels. He may give you a fresh revelation of his unfathomable love that transforms you.

A prophet's reward means *greater encounters*. By definition, an encounter is something you didn't expect. You never saw it coming. God will surprise and delight his faithful honorable ones with the weighty *kāḇôḏ* of his presence in places and contexts that are unexpected—even startling! He will meet you right where you are and fill you with more of himself to the point of overflowing. He will bless you to be a blessing to others on this unfolding pathway of honor to a prophet's reward. Wait for it: he's about to blow your mind! The treasures in store for you are also quite practical for your life on earth here and now. The prophet's reward includes enhanced benefits in the natural world that are brought on by supernatural means.

A prophet's reward means *open doors.* I may sound like a broken record at this point, but God's open-door policy translates to the natural world! Walk in honor, and you'll see practical, tangible opportunities open up that you never could have forced your way into. For me, this looked like more invitations to travel, teach, and minister around the globe, as well as sponsorships, notoriety, and fame within the kingdom. For you, it might look like job openings, start-up funding for a big business idea, or simply being at the right place at the right time to get a foot in the door to where you want to go. When you walk in honor, doors swing open wide!

A prophet's reward means *kingdom connections.* In the latter part of the twentieth century, sociology researchers theorized that all people on earth are six or fewer social connections away from each other. These "six degrees of separation," also referred to in Hollywood-movie-star circles as the "six degrees from Kevin Bacon,"[26] assume that we are no more than five or six relationships away from connecting to someone who could reshape our lives.[27] If you don't know the right person? Someone you know knows someone who does, within six people. Friend, I'm here to tell you that in the kingdom of God we have only two degrees of separation—you to the Holy Spirit to literally any man or woman of God you need access to! There is no scarcity in the kingdom, nor are there communication or logistics issues that God cannot overcome. If you need to know someone? God can and will make an introduction.

A prophet's reward means *increased authority.* Positioning yourself to claim your kingdom inheritance and prophet's rewards won't make your life any easier. In fact, each promotion you receive will come with increased authority and an expanded calling to shepherd the flock more actively. While your life won't be easy, you will be able to live life with ease—leaning into a peace that passes understanding (Philippians 4:6–7). Even in conflict. Even in persecution. Even in martyrdom. Stephen, the first martyr of the church, echoed the words of Jesus as he prayed for his own attackers (Acts 7:59–60).[28] The unlikely prophet "Uncle Ben" Parker paraphrased Sir Winston Churchill's famous 1906 speech when he spoke to his nephew Peter Parker (a.k.a. the Amazing Spider-Man), and these words ring true when it comes to honor: "With great power comes great responsibility."[29] I might add to that, "With great power comes great authority."

Receiving a prophet's reward comes with some profoundly beautiful strings attached. When you are equipped with a greater measure of reward, God will move you with compassion to do signs, wonders, miracles, and other good works you would never be able to say yes to in your own strength. But with the power of the Holy Spirit living in you and a full treasure trove of heaven's resources at your disposal, you, my friend, won't just seek the kingdom; you will bring it here and now, on earth as it is in heaven. It's what you were always meant to do and who you were created to be—an honorable image-bearer of the Most High God.

Discerning a True Prophet

A big question remains when it comes to honoring a prophet to receive a prophet's reward. Can we, in all humility and humanness, rightfully discern a true prophet from a false prophet? I believe we can. Why would the Lord give such rich rewards for honoring prophets if we were unable to recognize them?

Admittedly, the church tends to focus more heavily on identifying (and then quickly disparaging) false prophets than on discerning true prophets. While discernment is necessary, we must be careful that our suspicion does not turn into a witch hunt! Such a conspiring self-righteousness far too often consumes God's true kingdom plans and activities. In our pride, it allows us to lord ourselves over others in a prophetic spirit in dishonor. We build our empirical "cities on a hill" and protect them from new ways of thinking, and then the true prophets rightfully leave town in response so they can find those who are truly hungry. This is why I would rather spend my time teaching what prophets do, not what they don't do. Let's look at four things prophets do: bear and share the fruit of the Spirit; engage in sound, balanced teaching; submit to the authority of Scripture; and adhere to a simple yet undiluted gospel.

Prophets bear and share the fruit of the Spirit. "But the fruit of the Spirit is love, joy, peace, patience, kindness, goodness, faithfulness, gentleness, self-control; against such things there is no law" (Galatians 5:22–23). Matthew 7 teaches us that we will be able to *discern* prophets by their fruit; it doesn't say we will *judge* them by their fruits (vv. 16–20). Good prophets will not only bear good fruit; they will also share it with hungry ones eager to taste and see just how good the Lord is! As you discern, be aware that your own preferences, tastes, and experiences can be limited. If you've only enjoyed apples and bananas, imagine how your eyes and your taste buds might react to the diverse sight and tastes of a papaya, a kumquat, or a persimmon. To say "this doesn't look or taste like an apple, so it must not be good" is foolishness! Same goes for the nine fruits of the Spirit, with their wide and delicious variations.

Prophets engage in sound, balanced teaching. God is not a God of confusion. He doesn't muddle, trick, or string his people along. He speaks to them plainly in ways that resonate well with their spirits. When God speaks through his prophets, his voice will sound like mercy, not judgment. Like compassion, not indifference. Like honor, grace, and peace, not wrath. Prophets won't take sides here on earth; they will remain a spiritual "Switzerland" of sorts (the country with the oldest policy of military neutrality in the world). They will seek unity and purity in all things, coming against anything that hinders these. A prophetic voice transcends age, race, nationality, politics, and culture—often bringing humbling and refining words of wisdom to transform our broken religious theologies and earthly ideologies into heaven's gospel truth. A true prophet will carry an anointing that's anything but shtick and will be able to build on sound doctrinal foundations with fresh, revelatory ways of looking at things, bringing hearts to repentance.

Prophets submit to the authority of Scripture. While a prophet may come in a spirit of unity, he or she will absolutely separate the wheat from the chaff in a particular community. A true prophet knows revelation is only revelation when it can be backed up in Scripture, not just experience. True prophets know the Word of God to be divinely inspired—and unfortunately, very humanly interpreted at times. They seek to bring clarity to Scripture with Scripture, and they know that any sign, wonder, or miracle God wants to do is an extension of the biblical truth he has given us in order to rule and reign in this world. A prophet will never deviate from biblical truth, only seek to bring enhanced clarity to what has always been true, with appropriate context and timing. A prophet will never seek to make a name for himself or herself—only for the One he or she represents. And by doing so faithfully, such a prophet will often be known throughout the world.

Prophets adhere to a simple yet undiluted gospel. Though they might be well-versed in a multitude of theological ideologies, a prophet will never "major in the minors," seeking to prioritize a doctrinal issue over the beauty of the gospel. Prophets stand for truth because they stand for Christ alone. They carry a message for the entire world, not just for the enlightened, the educated, or the elite. They will walk in honor in the way of Jesus—dining with sinners and upsetting the religious establishment. They'll be loved and hated. They'll be accepted and rejected. They'll be honored and outright attacked. (I know, because I have been.) But a true prophet will uncompromisingly cling to the good news, knowing there's no need to embellish it, water it down, or compromise on its truth for any reason. And the truest test? They'll be willing to die to make sure everyone they encounter knows how deeply God loves each and every one of us.

An All-Access Pass

When you honor a prophet in your home and your community at large, the grace on that particular prophet's life can and will be transported to you. The prophet's history, blessing, and rewards become readily available to you as part of your shared birthright in Christ—without taking a single blessing or reward away from the prophet! That prophet's harvest becomes your inheritance, and you begin to win souls together, in partnership, for the good of the kingdom.

When you honor a prophet, you come into the history and blessings the prophet has. It's an all-access pass to the treasure troves of heaven. And the beautiful part? A true prophet will be thrilled to share these kingdom resources with you because he or she knows there's no scarcity in the Lord's kingdom. We can receive unique, dynamic graces in our lives when we remain open to receive.

I've encountered a precious crew of these true prophets in my day, and they continue to shape my walk of honor in this realm. When I've honored them, I've received double honor in return. The prophets themselves not only richly blessed me with their presence, influence, and connections; they also opened the door for me to receive from the Lord on a whole new level.

You honor each person differently, staying sensitive to the person's liking. I once sowed and blessed an evangelist, giving him the biggest financial seed I've ever planted. After this act of honor, my context for miracles increased exponentially. But even more, the joy of the Lord in my ministry—his very presence in my meetings—increased exponentially. Because I honored a prophet, there was a direct impartation of his gifts in my life. This is the prophet's reward.

Because I honored a prophet, there was a direct impartation of his gifts in my life. This is the prophet's reward.

Does this instant manifestation of rewards happen all the time? My goodness gracious, no. But it does happen. When you want to go to a higher level, you receive it by honoring those who go before you. It takes humility. You're not all that and a bag of chips. There is always someone who carries more. You're not automatically better than the people around you. When you humble yourself, blessing a man or woman of God, you will receive compounded blessings continually. When you sow into someone, you will reap from the blessing he or she carries. I've seen it and experienced it time and again. If you want to increase, *bless*.

Consider the book you hold in your hands right now. The publishing deal was not only because of my perseverance, but because I've sown into bestselling authors—loving, befriending, and honoring them—believing that the same grace might touch my own life, Lord willing. Whether this book becomes my first on *The New York Times* bestseller list or a wildly controversial sacred work hidden away by the prophets for fear of God's message being commoditized, I have been richly favored and blessed—and God will be honored because of the words he gave me to share with you.

Embracing the Simple Gospel

Receiving a prophet's reward demands a level of humility that I dare say today's church does not teach. No matter how hard you try, you can't snatch a mantle from a prophet passing by. Sure, you can ask for it, as Elisha did, and it will fall to you in God's perfect timing when you choose to walk in honor. But believing the lie that there's some level of holiness to achieve to be worthy will keep you stuck at your current level.

You see, receiving a prophet's reward isn't about knowledge, skill, or achievements. No amount of right thinking or perfected doctrine will manifest it. It comes only when you walk in honor, receiving prophets with an open heart and mind from wherever God may have sent them. The westernized American church has embraced a spirit of division that I believe is from the deepest pit of hell. Catholics and Protestants; Wesleyans and Calvinists; charismatics and evangelicals. Denominationalism was never a biblical idea; it was a man-made one—resulting in a man-made, commoditized, and consumer-driven church that is failing. Just as one example, research shows that there may be as many as two hundred different types of Baptists out there,[30] each respective persuasion either unwilling or unable to seek out the common ground of Christ in our midst—the simple beauty of the gospel that unites us all. I dare say that our first days in heaven are going to be a little awkward if we can't first learn to honor one another in this realm.

We're already one with God in Christ by the power of the Holy Spirit, which makes us all one with each other. We just don't know it yet. Or even if we do, we're not sure we want to believe it yet, because we'd rather be "right" than redeeming.

Now, don't hear what I'm not saying. I believe in absolute truth and the absolute inerrancy of Holy Scripture. I also believe in mankind's finite attempt to interpret the Word of an infinite God. God is God, and we are not. And if we're honest, we'll admit that much of the division the church is facing today has little (if anything) to do with Scripture and everything to do with tradition.

Pride is a harsh mistress; she'll do anything to keep you out of right relationship with other believers. While I would never ask you to compromise truth by caving on your "perfected" doctrine, I might ask you to consider these questions:

- If God asked you to tweak your theology, would you be willing or able to do it?
- Do you worship the Triune God or some bizarre, man-made version of him?
- If God brought clarity to Scripture that meant you'd been "doing it wrong," would you admit it and repent?

When we cling to our ideologies too tightly, we risk missing out on revelation that's meant for this moment, this generation. The Word of God is as alive as he is—and the Lord is still speaking through it! It's because of this truth that we must learn to discern a prophet. Prophets may not look, think, act, worship, or interpret Scripture exactly the way we do. In fact, I dare say that's the whole point. When God wants to speak words of revelation, correction, or even activation, it's not going to look, sound, or feel like anything we've seen, heard, or felt before. Part of entertaining prophets is staying hungry. Instead of obsessing over what makes them different (and thereby potentially dangerous), stay focused on what unites you. Do they come in peace? Do they walk in humility? Have they resolved to know nothing but Christ and him crucified (1 Corinthians 2:2)? These are powerful reasons not only to stay in the room, but also to gather at the table to break bread with one another. Denominationalism is done away with. Having a kingdom focus dictates that it's time we come together in the powerful name of Jesus and love people.

I believe a huge opportunity exists for millennials, Gen Zers, and beyond to foster a spirit of union in the body of Christ. While unity is all too often a front for uniformity, union allows us to embrace the beauty and diversity in the kingdom of God—and yes, even some of our toughest theological debates—so long as they don't detract from the simple gospel. I am believing for a future where denominations reject a spirit of competition in the kingdom and honor one another in our respective collective races. Debates like transubstantiation versus consubstantiation, pre-tribulation versus post-tribulation, and even traditional versus contemporary worship styles will one day fade away. We can honor our elders, our denominational contemporaries, and even our disciples fully (even when we don't agree!) by seeking first to understand where they are coming from rather than trying to correct their thinking. No more one-upmanship. No more black hat, white hat. No more manufactured mantles. Only a willingness to receive the mantle, continue the race, and pass the torch throughout the generations. Honor is our only way forward.

Receiving Honor, Glory, and Blessing

If receiving a prophet's reward is the ultimate honor in the kingdom, bestowing honor on the prophets must be our top priority. This brings honor to God and to his people, and it ultimately brings honor on us as well. We can receive more from God when we learn to receive his grace gifts—gifts of unmerited favor that we can't possibly earn in our own strength. The more we receive, the more we are able to give. The more we give, the more we are able to receive. And the One who is worthy of all honor and glory and blessing (Revelation 5:12) would like nothing more than to share them with you.

Honoring solely to be honored isn't honor at all. It's narcissism. It requires spiritual discipline on our part to remain selfless and pure as we walk in honor for the sake of the world. So stay hungry. Stay teachable. Stay humble. Stay open. Stay kind. Commit to destroying any willful ignorance in your life, anything that might keep you from receiving a prophet due to prideful misunderstanding. God's people are destroyed when they reject knowledge (Hosea 4:6). So it's up to us to remember again to reclaim the lost art of honor in our generation and to preserve it for our children and their children and their children.

The big question—and a fitting one for the last pages of a book that I hope will change everything about the way you look at honor and at yourself in Christ—is *Are you ready?*

You must not try to receive something if you're not ready to respond. It will cost you everything. Before you can finance a tower, you need to count the cost. And you should do it before the building starts, not after (Luke 14:28–30). Only you know where you stand when it comes to honor. Let me ask you these questions:

- Are you walking out the Lord's call on your life?
- Have you committed to living life unoffendable?
- Are you receiving prophets and experiencing a prophet's reward?
- If not, are you ready to do so?

If you are someone who is ill, I also want to ask you some other questions:

- Do you *want* to be healed (John 5:6)?
- Are doubt, depression, or disillusion keeping you from the healing that's right in front of you, much like Jesus stood before the leper at the pool in Bethesda and the leper didn't recognize him as the healer that he was (vv. 1–15)?
- Are you more comfortable wallowing in doubt, self-pity, or offense because it's all you know?

If you are ill, resist the temptation to list all the reasons why you're either unable or unwilling to be healed on your own. The Lord already knows that. But as his gentle, compassionate whisper asks you, *Child, do you want to be healed?* (John 5:6), give him your yes—and let him get to work on the details.

Now, being cleansed and healed is one thing. But will you give God the honor, glory, and blessing he is due for it? In Luke 17, Jesus healed ten lepers who were more than willing, but only one of them—a Samaritan, at that—returned to thank him:

> And one of them, when he saw that he was healed, returned, and with a loud voice glorified God, and fell down on his face at His feet, giving Him

> thanks. And he was a Samaritan.
>
> So Jesus answered and said, "Were there not ten cleansed? But where are the nine? Were there not any found who returned to give glory to God except this foreigner?" And He said to him, "Arise, go your way. Your faith has made you well." (vv. 15–19)

Scripture implies that the other nine were indeed healed on the way to show their newfound cleanliness to the priests (v. 14). It doesn't say they were not healed or that the healing was somehow revoked because of their lack of gratitude. They were healed, but were they saved? They were delivered from disease, but were their hearts moved? They were ritually clean in the eyes of religious authorities, but were they made perfect, holy, and blameless before God—equipped and empowered to do his works? We may never know, this side of heaven. But one thing is clear: The Samaritan who returned to Christ to give him the honor that was due positioned himself to receive a prophet's reward. The others may have been delivered from leprosy, but the honorable man received a far superior gift of freedom given to him by his Master.

The lesson here is that gifts from the Lord demand a response. We must take immediate action, like the Samaritan former leper did, even if it means making the religious leaders wait to verify if you've really been cleansed. Otherwise, the healing may be good for what it is, but it won't equip you to level up in your kingdom life!

If you're still struggling to embrace honor as a biblical imperative, you likely have more inner healing to do. I can sense that a few will scoff at this, thinking, *I've done my work. God already healed me.* Or my personal favorite, *Look, I run such and such a ministry at my church, Ben—so you can chill.* Lay down your pride. Be still.

Honestly assess your life and ask the Lord to reveal anything in you that's not of him—anything that would hinder you from walking in honor as his image-bearer. Pride. Unforgiveness. Lust. Greed. Hate. Fear. Whatever it is, acknowledge it to the Lord. Name it, even if you're not exactly sure what to do with it, and ask him to move powerfully on your behalf. Say to your Maker, *I believe! Lord, help my unbelief!* (Mark 9:24).

God will reward your humility, receive your honorable requests, and cleanse you of all unrighteousness, equipping you to be an ambassador of honor within your spheres of influence. You don't have to grasp the healing intellectually. God's ways are mysterious, and they rarely "make sense" in the moment. Just receive your healing in the Spirit.

As we come to a close, ask yourself:

- *Am I willing to receive this prophetic message about honor?*
- *Am I willing to receive this author—an admittedly unusual, underdog prophet?*
- *Am I willing to reclaim the lost art of honor in my own life and ministry?*

If your answer is yes to all three questions, then surely you will reap—and heap—the double portion of honor that comes with a prophet's reward! Honor will bring healing, wholeness, and blessing—more than you could ever ask for or imagine in a thousand lifetimes. May you find it and also reclaim it for your generation, my friend.

Allow your God to share with you the fullness of your inheritance—which includes the honor, glory, and blessing of which only he is worthy. When you do, you'll start to see yourself the way he sees you—as the honorable, righteous image-bearer you always have been, and Lord willing, always will be. And once you see yourself as God sees you? You might even start to believe it's true. You might begin living a lifestyle of kingdom honor that brings hope, healing, and restoration throughout the generations, in Jesus' name. Amen and amen.

Honorable Reflections

Is the prophet's reward for everybody?

Have you ever received a prophet's reward?

How could you approach discerning a prophet in the Spirit?

Have you ever dishonored or wrongfully dismissed a true prophet?

If everybody can receive a prophet's reward, what holds some of us back?

Afterword: Honor Activations and Declarations

First, let me take a moment to honor you, faithful reader, for making it all the way to the end of my book, *The Supernatural Power of Honor*. Thank you from the bottom of my heart. You've no doubt "felt all the feels" as you've received my invitation and challenge when it comes to honor—and if you're still reading, you're likely looking for some intensely practical honor applications and activations in your own life. I won't disappoint you.

If you're going to reclaim the lost art of honor in your generation, bridging the ever-widening gap in the church and society as a whole, you're going to need prophetic covering. Humble as it might be, this afterword is designed to cover *you* under my prophetic authority as you establish honor as a key tool in your tool kit. Perhaps you already know me personally, or perhaps you don't know me from Adam. Either way, I'm committed to covering you in prayer as you step into the unique honor anointing that is being passed down from me to you.

These prophetic activations are for you, to equip and empower you as you step out in faith and walk in honor. You're not doing it because you have to. At some level, I know you're doing it because you want to, and I want to honor the gold being mined in your spirit. You won't walk out honor perfectly, so give yourself some grace in this trial-and-error season of adoption. The point is that you've heard from the Lord, you want to be obedient to his call, and you're looking for a way forward.

This afterword isn't just for you, by the way. It's for your family, your church, your workplace, and your community. It's for the ones you love and lead, and it's for the ones who love and lead you. Whether we are hungry or entitled, gracious or withholding, these humble prayers are for *all* of us—image-bearers of the Most High God who have yet to come into their own.

> *God, help us. Humble us. Hear our prayers as we seek to honor you. You alone are worthy of all honor and glory and blessing.*

Embracing Honor

This activation is for the skeptics, the cynics—the ones who flipped through the pages of this book and said, "That's nice, but I can't imagine it being relevant in my own life and ministry."

May the grace of God open your heart and mind to receive "the lost art of honor" in humility. May the life situations keeping you from embracing honor as a biblical imperative be shaken up in the best of ways—brought to a head by the righteous right hand of your Father in heaven. Let me declare over you,

> *Entitlement, be gone, in the powerful name of Jesus. Offense, find your rightful place in hell and go there to stay. Relational discord, resolve and change your tune right now, in the name of our Lord Jesus.*
>
> *Lord, anything this dear one is clinging to now that's not of you, may it be revealed. God, make it*

obvious what's holding your servant, your image-bearer, back from the glory you intended for his or her life.

Pause now and name anything that comes to mind that could be holding you back. Next, declare these words over yourself with the authority God has given you in Christ by the power of the Spirit:

God, I receive your mantle of honor—one I was created to carry for my generation. I admit that I'm not strong enough to carry it on my own. I need your help, Lord. Give me strength to combat offense and extend the olive branch as you would. Help me walk in honor even when it gets hard. Especially then. I know deep down that I am meant for more than I even think I am. Show me what your way of honor looks like in my life. Help me reclaim it in my generation and bridge the gaps causing distance and separation among your people. Thank you, Lord, for this rich blessing of honor. In Jesus' name. Amen.

And every creature which is in heaven and on the earth and under the earth and such as are in the sea, and all that are in them, I heard saying:

> "Blessing and honor and glory and power
> Be to Him who sits on the throne,
> And to the Lamb, forever and ever!"
> (Revelation 5:13)

Honoring the Hard One

This activation is for the reluctant ones—the ones who know deep down that honor is due to someone, but in their pride, they simply can't figure out how to bestow it in their own strength. God sees you. He sees your situation, and he knows how hard the way of honor can be. Humility is not for the faint of heart, and the good news is, he made your heart strong and vibrant, ready to be moved with compassion to do his will.

I hear the Lord asking, *Are you willing to look like a fool for the gospel—or not? Are you willing to honor the gold in all people, even if you have to dig deep to find it?*

Brother, are you willing? Sister, are you ready? Whoever it is that you just can't bring yourself to honor right now, I plead the blood of Jesus over your heart, mind, body, soul, spirit, and will. Whatever has happened, whatever has been done to you, I declare peace over the relational storm in Jesus' name. The Lord is inviting you to go deeper, to reach higher, to find *something* you can honor in this individual. Perhaps your father abandoned you in childhood, but at least he gave you life. Perhaps your elder dishonored you publicly, but at least he or she laid a firm foundation for you to build on. Perhaps your former spouse lied and cheated and left, but at least he or she is a devoted parent to your shared children.

Swallow your pride. If you make an honest effort, you can find something to honor in everyone—because we were all created in the image of God. His divine DNA is unmistakable. Even Hitler himself, arguably one of the worst human beings who ever walked the earth, was one of the most powerful military strategists the world has ever seen. Imagine if he had been open to gentle (and not-so-gentle) nudges from the Holy Spirit that might have sent his passion and fervor in right directions? This is what's on the table for leaders at all levels in our day—even you. Let's ask in prayer,

> *God, humble your servants to honor the ones right in front of them. Teach us to honor the divine DNA in each person—even when we don't want to or don't know how to. Teach us to hear your voice, live by grace, and walk in honor—no matter what.*

> Obey those who rule over you, and be submissive, for they watch out for your souls, as those who must give account. Let them do so with joy and not with grief, for that would be unprofitable for you. (Hebrews 13:17)

Honor Where Honor Isn't Felt

This activation is for the ones who hoped to receive honor but have had to go without. The dissonance in your spirit over dis honor is a righteous dissonance. That's because when honor is withheld, it goes against the very nature and character of God.

Perhaps you are an emerging leader whose ideas have been dismissed by the very elders meant to pass you the torch. Perhaps you are an elder whose reluctant disciples refuse to acknowledge the trails you blazed for them in the kingdom—the rights, opportunities, and freedoms you won for them, which they now take for granted. Perhaps honor was bestowed on you but not in the method or measure you expected, causing pain and confusion in your relationships. Or perhaps your prophetic voice fell on deaf ears in your own home church, hometown, or home country. My friend, you aren't the first. And unless we reclaim the lost art of honor in our generation, you won't be the last. So I declare over you,

> *Father, we declare your righteous peace over every heart and mind in this situation. We seek first to understand, not be understood; we seek first to love, not be loved; we seek first to honor, not be honored. Take us twenty thousand leagues deeper into humility, Lord. When necessary, teach us what it means to be despised and rejected by man. In learning humility your way, make us more powerful conduits of honor from this day on. Make us better so we can honor better.*
>
> *And Father, reveal a deeper measure of your delight for this overlooked, underappreciated child of yours. Honor him or her before man, as your Word says. Bring your servant's contributions into the light. Let this one claim your honor as his or her own and share in the glory and blessing that is part of our inheritance in Christ. Whether in this realm or the next, let honor flow like a river into the eternal life of this precious one. May he or she seek your face above all else.*

"I do not receive honor from men. But I know you, that you do not have the love of God in you."
(John 5:41–42 NKJV)

Breaking Off Dishonor

This activation is for the ones who are either eager to dispel dishonor or clueless that they are steeped in it. When dishonor hangs in the atmosphere, it can impact every interaction we might have with men and women of God. The church has tolerated dishonor for far too long, breeding it throughout the generations. If honor is a lost art, it's up to us to reclaim it by coming against dishonor in the powerful and mighty name of Jesus. So I declare over you,

> *With the power and authority given to me by our Lord and Savior, Jesus Christ, and by the power of the Spirit living within me, I declare that dishonor cease within your community cultures and circles of influence. I break the calcified damage of dishonor off your life—off your heart, mind, body, spirit, soul, and will. I come against anything and anyone opposing honor in your life, purifying your heart completely from words of poison spoken over you in dishonor. May anything dishonorable that's been said or even been thought against you evaporate into the atmosphere until there is nothing left. I come against word curses, generational curses, curses to your good name—any curse that may have caused you to believe you are less than honorable, or that you are less than honoring.*
>
> *From this day forward, you will cling to your identity as an image-bearer of your Creator God, designed to be a vessel of honor for his kingdom in this realm. May you never again question who you are, and may your walk with the Lord be a walk of*

honor that brings about glory and blessing to him and to the ones you love and lead.

> But above all, my brethren, do not swear, either by heaven or by earth or with any other oath. But let your "Yes" be "Yes," and your "No," "No," lest you fall into judgment. (James 5:12 NKJV)

Honor in a Family of Origin

This activation is for the ones who struggle to show honor within their family of origin. "Honor your father and mother" seems like such a basic commandment, but the sentiment carries heavy baggage for so many. Whether the dishonor lies with a dad or mom, brother or sister, aunt or uncle, or anyone who may have been responsible for bringing you into and/or bringing you up in this world, it's time to bring peace by reestablishing an honor baseline in your family.

When family dishonor festers, the Lord is grieved. As a perfect Father, he designed the family unit to be a physical representation of the Trinity—Father (represented by dads), Son (represented by children), and Holy Spirit (represented by moms). Perhaps your family dishonored you. Perhaps you dishonored them. Perhaps it's a long-standing, reciprocal spiritual battle for the ages, steeped in your own shared bloodline. Whatever your reasons, no matter what has happened, you can choose to honor members of your family of origin without compromising your safety, your mental health, or your spirit.

So take a moment with your heavenly Father now. Ask him to reveal specific points of dishonor and defensiveness between you and your family. Ask him to show you the very real wrongs that have been done as well as any perceived wrongs that may need to be addressed and clarified. Also ask him to show you your part, if any, in the offenses.

Now go ahead and count the costs of the dishonor in your family. What has it cost you? Your relationships? Your safety? Your support system? Your mental and emotional health? Be bold and honest, acknowledging what a spirit of dishonor has done.

Next, think of the person or people within your family of origin who offended or dishonored you in some way. Person by person, find one single, simple thing that you can honor about each individual. Before you give up on this exercise, realize that honoring an individual does not mean excusing his or her offenses against you. Bestowing honor can be a humble first step toward forgiveness that frees you. Give it a try. Perhaps your abusive father had a strong work ethic that he passed on to you. Perhaps your emotionally absent mother still gave birth to you and raised you the best she knew how. Perhaps an estranged sibling stood up for you once in childhood, in a way that still sticks with your spirit. Whatever it is, no matter how small, find something in your offender that you can honor, even in that person's humanity. Pause now and speak words of honor over your family member.

Let's now pray this together:

> *Lord, we know all it takes is a tiny crack for the walls you want to come down to crumble. We praise you and glorify your name for what you are already doing in this dear reader's heart and mind. Thank*

you for your gifts of mercy, forgiveness, and unmerited favor. Your grace astounds and inspires us to want to be more and more like you. Father, we come against dishonor in this one's family now, in the powerful and mighty name of Jesus. We declare peace, deeper understanding, restoration, and reconciliation here and now, on earth as it is in heaven.

Moreover, we come against a spirit of division that would seek to destroy the godly family unit in society. May father be reunited to son, mother to daughter, brother to sister, and so on—all through us embracing honor and stepping into their roles as vessels of honor on the earth for the kingdom.

And God, even when reconciliation is not safe or possible, we declare your peace as a shift in the atmosphere that will change family dynamics and relationships forever, in Jesus' name. May honor reign supreme.

Children, obey your parents in the Lord, for this is right. "Honor your father and mother," which is the first commandment with promise: "that it may be well with you and you may live long on the earth."

And you, fathers, do not provoke your children to wrath, but bring them up in the training and admonition of the Lord. (Ephesians 6:1–4 NKJV)

Honor in Marriage

This activation is for the ones bold enough and brave enough to enter into a holy covenant of marriage—a covenant designed to emulate our covenant with the Lord. Oh, how we humans have misunderstood marriage. What started as a pledge to oneness has turned into mere contractual obligation, with husbands and wives more apt to call it quits than honor a "for better or worse" promise. So I declare over you now,

> *To our own Bridegroom King, bring back honor to marriage, which has all but lost honor in the eyes of humanity in our day. To the dishonored husband, bring back full honor and respect. To the dishonored wife, bring back full honor and respect. Teach us the beauty of mutual submission—a wife who loves her husband more than she loves herself and a husband who loves his wife so much that he'd die for her, as Christ died for us. Lord, teach us what true covenant means by way of your everlasting covenant with us in the shed blood of Jesus, the perfect, spotless Lamb.*
>
> *Where betrayal has crept in, Lord, renew trust. Where superiority has elevated one spouse over another, Lord, restore balance. Where resentment and avoidance have exacerbated problems, Lord, restore healthy, productive communication. Where abuse, abandonment, and a spirit of narcissism have reigned, Lord, restore safety, intimacy, and selflessness.*
>
> *Lord, we know that what you bring together,*

no one can rip apart (Matthew 19:6). As we cling to our oneness with you, God, teach husbands and wives to cling to a "one flesh" reality with their kingdom life partners, chosen by you since before the foundations of the earth. (I do believe you have predestined connections for us, but help us do our part not to sabotage, miss, or destroy those.) Equip these precious couples, Lord, with shared kingdom work that they need one another to accomplish.

> Wives, submit to your own husbands, as to the Lord…Husbands, love your wives, just as Christ also loved the church and gave Himself for her. (Ephesians 5:22, 25)

Honor in the Workplace

This activation is for the ones called to the ministry of work—or the work of ministry. Your workplace, whether in your cozy home office or atop a skyscraper in a major metro, is a place primed for conflict and dishonor. When subordinates and supervisors feel more like slaves and masters, it can be risky business showing honor in the midst of disagreement. But it's the way of the kingdom. When dishonor might cost you your livelihood, it's critical to lean into the Father's kingdom principles.

Friend, the Lord wants you to know you are worthy of your hire, as are all who enter the workforce with humility, resourcefulness, and a strong work ethic. As employees, we honor our employers and clients by operating with excellence, to the best of our abilities. As employers, we honor our employees, contractors, and customers by setting reasonable and fair expectations and following through on promises. Whether you work for someone or have someone working for you, reclaiming honor in the workplace will dramatically bless everyone involved.

Unfortunately, the workplace can also be a breeding ground for dishonor because the cutthroat nature of commerce is counter to the kingdom. That said, if you are called to be *in* the world but not *of* it (John 17:14–16), live by an honor code you won't compromise for selfish gain. This will get you far in the natural and the supernatural world. So let's declare over our workplaces,

> *Father, we come against both tyranny and apathy in the workplace, in Jesus' name. May each worthy hire understand the value of his or her pearls, refusing to cast them before swine. May each one called to love and lead in the workplace be ready to surprise and delight hard workers with precious gems and rubies—promotions, bonuses, corner offices, and above all, recognition. May work be our mission field, whether that's a literal mission field or the mission field of Wall Street. Teach us to do your good work whenever, wherever, and with whomever we are called to, in Jesus' name.*
>
> *Lord, infuse honor into the halls of commerce where we work. Bless individuals, organizations, communities, and even nations for our good and for your glory. Lord, keep us humble as we work. Keep us passionate and creative. Keep us not just hopeful*

but hope-filled to overflowing. Unlock kingdom secrets that will change the way the world of work works forever and ever. Amen.

> Bondservants, be obedient to those who are your masters according to the flesh, with fear and trembling, in sincerity of heart, as to Christ; not with eyeservice, as men-pleasers, but as bondservants of Christ, doing the will of God from the heart, with goodwill doing service, as to the Lord, and not to men, knowing that whatever good anyone does, he will receive the same from the Lord, whether he is a slave or free.
>
> And you, masters, do the same things to them, giving up threatening, knowing that your own Master also is in heaven, and there is no partiality with Him. (Ephesians 6:5–9 NKJV)

Honor in the Church

This activation is for the self-proclaimed "deconstructors"—the trauma-laden, wounded souls who have been, in one way or another, dishonored, disserved, or disenfranchised by the bride of Christ. My heart is moved with compassion for you, beloved friend. What was meant to be a safe haven and sanctuary for you has become a place of discrimination, marginalization, confusion, and judgment. I pray for you and for all of us in the church,

Lord, have mercy on us. In our humanity, we have taken your church and made an idol of it—embracing man-made systems, structures, and ministry silos or wineskins that breed hypocrisy. Forgive us. Show us the way to true reform, the way of honor.

Father, show us what is working well in your church and teach us to do more of it—anything that wins souls, brings healing, and equips your saints for the work of the kingdom. Show us also what is not working well and teach us either to reform it or release it—anything that perpetuates a country club mentality over being a refuge for the broken, the hungry, the desperate. Lord, show us what more we could do: new things we might try or even new ways of doing old things. Open our minds and soften our hearts to receive your Word through your prophets. Help us suspend disbelief and lean into the heavy revelation of honor you wish to bestow on us.

Where there is deconstruction, Father, through your Spirit lay out the plans to rebuild. Deconstruction without reconstruction is simply destruction. And we know that this cannot be the way forward for your church, your bride. Teach us to show honor, even in disagreement. Teach us to serve no matter the circumstance. Teach us to repent, believe, and do better as a body of believers. Teach us to live like Jesus and break our hearts for your people. Teach us to reconstruct your church your way—in the righteous way of honor.

> Jesus answered and said to them, "Destroy this temple, and in three days I will raise it up."
>
> Then the Jews said, "It has taken forty-six years to build this temple, and will You raise it up in three days?"
>
> But He was speaking of the temple of His body. Therefore, when He had risen from the dead, His disciples remembered that He had said this to them; and they believed the Scripture and the word which Jesus had said. (John 2:19–22 NKJV)

Honor in Divorce

This activation is for the ones who have loved and lost, the ones who have dreamed big dreams with another person that came crashing down around them. God hates divorce. But he does not hate *the divorced.* No matter the circumstances that led to a covenant broken, God does not brand you with a scarlet letter. No matter what happened, if you are in Christ, he sees you as pure and holy and blameless—not because of what you've done, but because of what Christ has done. In the Father's kingdom, there is a place for honor even in the aftermath of divorce. There is even space for relational restoration that transcends your wildest dreams. So I pray for you,

> *Father, give us an outpouring of honor over broken marriages today. In the dissonance of dividing a life, in the complexities of co-parenting, give us grace to*

handle the undeniable pain that comes with a broken covenant. Teach us what love after marriage looks like: healthy boundaries, clarified expectations, space and grace for your ex's humanity—and for yours too.

Father, it is most often through our failures that you make us better. And in our weakness, your strength is made perfect. We go through what we go through so we can help others go through what we went through. May love, respect, and peace in the aftermath of divorce be a testament to your goodness—even in the inevitability of pain in this life.

Never pay back evil with more evil. Do things in such a way that everyone can see you are honorable. Do all that you can to live in peace with everyone. (Romans 12:17–18 NLT)

Honor in Moral Failure

This activation is for the ones who have "fallen from grace" and also the ones who have been hurt by those who fell. When brute-strength morality alone fails us and we become all-too-comfortable with compromise, there will be consequences. No matter what you've done or how hard you've fallen, you'll find that the Lord's grace and mercy are limitless; they flow from a deep well that will never run dry. No matter how dire the situation, no matter how fierce the consequences, there is still grace to you and through you in the aftermath of moral failure.

Perhaps you are a leader who was put so high up on a pedestal that you were bound to fall eventually. When people worship the ground you walk on, you can start to believe the lie of your own deity. You thought yourself invincible, or perhaps you didn't think much about the consequences of your actions. Friend, there is grace for you.

Perhaps you witnessed a leader fall so abruptly, so unexpectedly, that it shook your own faith and resolve as a result. Perhaps you were a victim or casualty of said fall, and the trauma of it all feels like more than you can bear. Friend, there is grace for you too. Whatever your circumstance, I want to pray and declare over you,

> *Lord, give us courage to stand in the gap when moral failure seeks to divide us. Teach us to cover our leaders appropriately without covering up for them—to be the iron that sharpens iron, ones who will guide them to repent and restore relationships. Teach us to come alongside and comfort victims and casualties of moral failure, acknowledging pain and working together toward restoration and even restitution when necessary. Teach us to hold one another to a higher moral standard—a standard no one is above by birthright, title, office, or stature. Keep us humble, Lord, and remind us that rising up in the kingdom means going low in the here and now.*
>
> *I plead the blood of Jesus over moral failure in this generation. May foolishness be avoided, and may mistakes be addressed quickly and thoroughly. I come*

against any system or structure that seeks to perpetuate dishonor that would affect or even destroy tomorrow, or that would introduce failure within our ranks. Far be it from us, Lord, to let our humanity get in the way of your honor, glory, and blessing. In you, we are pure. In you, we are holy. In you, we are righteous. Help us believe that this is true.

> Now to Him who is able to keep you from stumbling, and to present you faultless before the presence of His glory with exceeding joy, to God our Savior, who alone is wise, be glory and majesty, dominion and power, both now and forever. Amen. (Jude 24–25)

Honor in Politics

This activation is for the righteous judge, the faithful advocate, the fierce activist—the one believing for a better world but who hasn't yet seen it or tasted it in his or her lifetime. The Lord is raising up a generation of change agents who transcend traditional political ideology and affiliation—the brave ones who aren't afraid to challenge the status quo, bring about much-needed reform, and cultivate a culture of honor in their own nations and around the world. So I ask in prayer over you,

Lord, protect us from the lies of the enemy, lies that would seek to divide those you have united in faith.

I come against political divisiveness in Jesus' name. I come against manipulation, greed, conceit, foolishness, and abuse of power. I come against selfishness, apathy, and a spirit of narcissism that might tempt us to overlook the log in our own eye to point out the speck in our brother's eye (Matthew 7:3). In the powerful name of Jesus, I come against a political spirit in my nation and every nation on earth.

Father, open our minds and soften our hearts to receive a spirit of honor in the political realm. May we learn honor in disagreement, faithfulness in our promises, and genuine compassion in our legislation. Your law is the only law that truly matters, and your law has been fulfilled in the person of Jesus Christ. May we learn to live under the new-covenant law of the Spirit and life, a law that enforces our oneness with God in Christ by the power of the Holy Spirit. May we be a generation willing to, in humility and love, bridge the gap instead of widening it. May we seek justice for the oppressed, opportunity for the willing, and peace for all of humankind, in Jesus' name.

May the words of our hearts, the meditations of our thoughts, and everything in between be not only acceptable but commendable in your sight, O Lord, our strength and Redeemer. May we learn to receive your prophets and taste the sweet fruit of a prophet's reward.

> You shall keep them, O Lord, you shall preserve them from this generation forever. The wicked prowl on every side, when vileness is exalted among the sons of men. (Psalm 12:7–8)

Honor in Community

This activation is for the ones who know deep down that we are better together. We were created for relationship with God and with one another. The clearest representation of the kingdom of God on earth is authentic Christian community. The sad reality is, we often confuse Christ-centered community with worldly community. We don't really want our people to show up as iron that sharpens iron (Proverbs 27:17); we want people who will feed our ego, entertain our gossip, affirm our offenses, and check all our boxes. Emotions are valid, and they can be helpful indicators of what's going on in our spirit. But the emotionally driven community of this world is not of the Lord. My prayer for all of us is therefore

> *Father, stir in your people a desire for authentic Christian community that will surround us and teach us to walk in honor individually and collectively. Embolden us to learn how to disciple others honorably, extending an open invitation and challenge for them to walk in the way of Jesus and drawing us all deeper into our knowledge of and love for you. By your Spirit, may we collectively harness the discipline it takes to give you honor, glory, and blessing by honoring others and honoring ourselves.*
>
> *Lord, in your authority, I break off any spirit of dishonor, disunity, or distraction in our communi-*

ties—anything that would seek to keep us from seeing who you are and who we are in you. Keep our eyes focused squarely on you. In your reflection in each other, as your image-bearers, may we learn to see the divine DNA that is worthy of honor in all people.

Lord, unleash a culture of honor within our communities. Teach us to reclaim the lost art of honor in our generation, laying a firm foundation for generations to come.

> And let us consider one another in order to stir up love and good works, not forsaking the assembling of ourselves together, as is the manner of some, but exhorting one another, and so much the more as you see the Day approaching. (Hebrews 10:24–25)

Honoring Yourself

We can't love and honor others as we love and honor ourselves unless we in fact honor ourselves. This critical component of identity is so often overlooked for fear that selfishness and self-righteousness will take hold. But my friend, you are an image-bearer of the Most High God. When he made you, he made you good. His divine DNA flows through your veins. As his beloved child, you are precious to him—and you carry unlimited value in the unmerited favor and grace of Jesus Christ.

Lord, I speak honor over this reader, who is your

vessel. I speak honor over your creation, honor over your beloved one.

Because you are a beloved image-bearer of God, in the end I want to say that you have to honor yourself in order to honor others. In fact, this is where you have to start if you're going to discover the breakthrough, fulfillment, restoration, and favor that come with the supernatural power of honor. You have to honor yourself (body, soul, name, and reputation) because you are a beloved representative of God himself on this earth. Let's look at how you honor yourself in each of these areas as we close. Consider how honoring yourself will honor your Creator and will enable you to honor the ones around you, whom he has also created and loves.

Dear one, honor your body. Your body is a temple of the Holy Spirit (2 Corinthians 16:19), fearfully and wonderfully made (Psalm 139:14). What if you were to love your body in words, thoughts, and actions—blessing it instead of cursing and judging it? Declare honor over your body and dedicate it, consecrate it as a temple of the Lord—a place where health is wealth and diversity and where all sizes and shapes are celebrated. It doesn't matter where your body has been or what it has been through—from this day forward, you are clean, pure, and holy before the Lord. You belong to God alone now, so walk in a manner where your body can be free from immorality, perversion, and sickness of any kind. You have been made new.

Dear one, honor your soul. Honor the essence of who you are in Christ and fiercely protect it—refusing to compromise it for human affections. I declare that you will learn to love yourself the way the Lord loves you, and that you will honor your own being as he honors you. You will value and protect your time, your gifts, your energy, and your presence—refusing to be devalued by toxic, manipulative, and/or religious people. You will not allow yourself to be put in situations that can bring you harm, destruction, or temptation. You are a vessel of honor; therefore, commit your life to the path of the cross. It is no longer you who live but Christ in you (Galatians 2:20). You are a bond servant to the Lord Jesus Christ, and your life is not your own. You will willingly obey Jesus no matter what, at all costs.

Dear one, honor your good name. I declare over you that your name is blessed and favored. A good name and reputation are worth more than gold and silver (Proverbs 22:1). Your name represents the name of God himself. He has a new name for you in him, and he knows you by it (Revelation 2:17). Your name is attached to blessing, prosperity, and destiny. Your name is blessed, honored, holy, true, and filled with love, light, and power. Your name will be remembered on earth as you lift up the name of Jesus Christ.

Now, read through the words of 1 Corinthians 13:4–7 that follow, replacing the word *love* with your own name. As a vessel of honor in this earthly realm, and by the grace of God, in time you will see that you *are* love.

__________ suffers long and is kind.
__________ does not envy.
__________ does not parade itself.
__________ is not puffed up.
__________ does not behave rudely.
__________ does not seek its own.
__________ is not provoked.
__________ thinks no evil.

__________ does not rejoice in iniquity but rejoices in the truth.

__________ bears all things.

__________ believes all things.

__________ hopes all things.

__________ endures all things.

In Christ, __________ conquers all.

Keep the honor flowing and discover breakthrough, fulfillment, restoration, and favor in the Lord Jesus Christ. #SupernaturalPowerofHonor

Acknowledgments

Pastor Benny and Momma Sue: thank you for your covering, your relationship, your grace, and for the impact of your ministry on my life.

My parents, “Papa and Mama Lim”: thank you for being my greatest supporters and most powerful intercessors.

My church, Open Heavens World: thank you, my family, for honoring me and offering my most foundational support.

Dolores of Rivera World Changers: thank you for being a great friend and media producer for our ministry.

Brit Eaton: thank you for your love, support, skill, and expository talent in the production of this book.

Dunamis Words: thank you for your covering and your continual belief in me as an author and minister of the gospel.

Don Milam: thank you for helping me shape this message and for believing I could be a published author.

My followers, supporters, and ministry partners: thank you for walking with me and believing in me.

Natasha Hinn: thank you for being a loving friend and sister when I needed you most.

And finally, “the haters”—the slanderers, the attackers, the dishonorable ones: thank you for helping me realize how badly the world needs this message.

About the Author

Dr. Ben Lim is the founder of Open Heavens World in Fountain Valley, California. A dynamic millennial preacher, he has traveled to nearly sixty countries over the last decade and a half since his born-again experience. He is also the founder and CEO of Ben Lim TV and Ben Lim Ministries. His ministry is accompanied by notable signs, wonders, and miracles.

Ordained by Pastor Benny Hinn and the World Healing Fellowship (WHF), Lim is a trusted voice and a regular feature on many prophetic streams and channels around the world. "God's glory is within you," he tells people, "and I'm here to help you activate it."

Lim spent his earlier years in the mission fields of Asia and Southeast Asia, preaching the gospel to unreached people groups. He has also ministered in evangelistic crusades in Pakistan, Dubai, and Africa, seeing hundreds of thousands come to Jesus. Today, he is known for his dynamic and life-changing preaching and revelations, along with his ministry, a family of kingdom-minded, cultivated hubs and communities which are sold-out for the gospel and are committed to seeing the good news walked out in every sphere of society, all across the earth. It is an end times ministry set on equipping those in the body of Christ, with their varied gifts and callings, to fulfill the Great Commission of the Lord.

Learn more about Dr. Ben Lim, his ministry, or Open Heavens World Church at www.benlimglobal.com.

Courses by Ben Lim

Dr. Ben Lim also offers a number of valuable online courses that will help you as you walk out a kingdom lifestyle as an image-bearer of God who reflects the supernatural power of honor. In addition, he offers a mentorship program for those who would like personalized mentoring, counseling, and discipleship. (The program includes options of group mentorship, one-on-one consultations, and elite or executive packages.) Learn more about the mentorship program and the courses at www.benlimglobal.com.

- **Supernatural Prosperity** — *a five-part e-course with Pastor Ben Lim and guest Dr. Roberts Liardon, author of the bestselling book series God's Generals.*
- **The Gift of Discernment** — *Pastor Ben Lim, Jamie Galloway, and Dr. Kynan Bridges teach this course on discernment.*
- **SOZO Inner Healing and Deliverance** — *features Dawna De Silva, Natasha Hinn, and Pastor Ben Lim as they impart revelation, restoration, and wholeness.*
- **School of Healing** — *Pastor Ben helps you understand more about the power of healing.*
- **School of Revival** — *Now is the time to rise up to bring revival! Pastor Ben teaches about the true meaning of revival.*

Endnotes

1 For more on this, see Jeff A. Benner, "The Philosophy of the Hebrew Language," Ancient Hebrew Research Center, https://www.ancient-hebrew.org.

2 Rabbi Shlomo Wolbe, as quoted by Rabbi David Jaffe in his website article "Kavod—Dignity," 2023, https://www.rabbidavidjaffe.com.

3 Blue Letter Bible, "*hāḏār*" (Strong's H1926), https://www.blueletterbible.org.

4 Blue Letter Bible, "*kāḇôḏ*" (Strong's H3519), https://www.blueletterbible.org.

5 Blue Letter Bible, "*timē*" (Strong's G5092), https://www.blueletterbible.org.

6 Blue Letter Bible, "*doxa*" (Strong's G1391), https://www.blueletterbible.org.

7 Breaking down the time spans for each generation in years is not an exact science. Sources vary about the specific years each generation includes, but here I have mostly followed Pew Research Center's breakdowns as found on the Library of Congress website listing the different generations. For more information, visit Library of Congress: Research Guides, "Generations," https://guides.loc.gov.

8 Tyler Baum, "Humans could live up to 150 years, new study claims," *New York Post*, March 27, 2022, https://nypost.com.

9 Louise Tickle, "Positive thinking can kill cancer cells, say psychologists," *The Guardian*, April 16, 2000, https://www.theguardian.com.

10 The wording in this bulleted list largely comes from the NKJV.

11 Nina McQueen, "Workplace culture trends: The key to hiring (and keeping) top talent in 2018," LinkedIn Official Blog, June 26, 2018, https://blog.linkedin.com.

12 Duke Haddad, EdD, "Job Satisfaction Depends upon Your Supervisor," NonProfit PRO, May 20, 2022, https://www.nonprofitpro.com.

13 *Merriam-Webster Dictionary*, "champion," https://www.merriam-webster.com.

14 Pew Research Center, "Modeling the Future of Religion in America," September 13, 2022, https://www.pewresearch.org.

15 David W. Jones, "Was Jesus Rich or Poor—and Why Does It Matter?," Center for Faith and Culture, July 7, 2016, https://cfc.sebts.edu.

16 *Cambridge Dictionary*, "integrity," https://dictionary.cambridge.org.

17 *Merriam-Webster Dictionary*, "truth," last updated March 2, 2025, https://www.merriam-webster.com.

18 *Britannica*, "Nicodemus," by Adam Zeidan, last modified August 7, 2023, https://www.britannica.com.

19 Blue Letter Bible, "*christos*" (Strong's G5547), https://www.blueletterbible.org.

20 Blue Letter Bible, "*chriō*" (Strong's G5548), https://www.blueletterbible.org.

21 This thought is taken from Jack Salzman and Cornel West, eds., *Struggles in the Promised Land: Toward a History of Black-Jewish*

Relations in the United States (Oxford University Press, 1997), n.p.

22 Pew Research Center, "In U.S., Decline of Christianity Continues at Rapid Pace," October 17, 2019, https://www.pewresearch.org.

23 D. E. Hiebert, *The Gospel of Mark: An Expositional Commentary* (Bob Jones University, 1994), 56.

24 James Brooks, *Mark*, The New American Commentary series, vol. 23 (Holman Reference, 1991), 100.

25 Randy Roberts, "Jinja, Uganda: Jinja for Jesus," Christ for all Nations Evangelistic Ministry, https://www.cfan.org.

26 David Greene, "The History Of 'Six Degrees of Kevin Bacon,'" NPR *Morning Edition*, September 14, 2012, https://www.npr.org.

27 Sanjita Rajesh Iyer, "The Evolution of Social Media: From Six Degrees to Facebook and Beyond," March 2, 2023, LinkedIn, https://www.linkedin.com.

28 *Britannica*, "St. Stephen: Christian martyr," last modified August 25, 2023, https://www.britannica.com.

29 *Wikipedia*, "With great power comes great responsibility," last modified August 25, 2023, https://en.wikipedia.org/wiki.

30 Amy Butler, "The Baptists, Part Three: Different Kinds of Baptists," *Talk with the Preacher* (blog), November 7, 2013, https://www.patheos.com/blogs/talkwiththepreacher.